Demystifying
Six Sigma

Demystifying Six Sigma

A Company-Wide Approach to Continuous Improvement

Alan Larson

AMACOM

American Management Association

New York • Atlanta • Brussels • Buenos Aires • Chicago • London • Mexico City
San Francisco • Shanghai • Tokyo • Toronto • Washington, D. C.

This publication is designed to provide accurate and authoritative information in regard to the subject matter covered. It is sold with the understanding that the publisher is not engaged in rendering legal, accounting, or other professional service. If legal advice or other expert assistance is required, the services of a competent professional person should be sought.

Library of Congress Cataloging-in-Publication Data

Larson, Alan.
    Six sigma demystified : a company-wide approach to continuous improvement / Alan Larson.
        p.   cm.
    Includes bibliographical references and index.
    ISBN 0-8144-7184-6
    1. Total quality management. 2. Six sigma (Quality control standard)
3. Customer services—Quality control. I. Title.
    HD62.15 .L372 2003
    658.4'013—dc21   2002152003

Printing number

10   9   8   7   6   5   4   3   2   1

CONTENTS

Preface   *ix*

SECTION ONE: THE BASICS OF SIX SIGMA   1

Chapter 1   The Grass Roots of Six Sigma   7
Why It Had to Be Invented   7
The Birth of Six Sigma   9
Black Belts and Green Belts   13
The Required Components   17
Notes   18

Chapter 2   Creating the Cultural Structure   19
Senior Management Roles and Engagement   19
Organizational Development   23
Requirements for Change   27
Note   31

Chapter 3   Preliminary Tasks   32
What Do You Want?   32
Selecting Projects   34
Collecting Data   37
Identifying Required Teams   37

Section Two: A Six Sigma Continuous
   Improvement Teaming Model   39

**Chapter 4   Step 1: Create the Operational Statement
   and Metric**   49
Operational Statement   49
Internal and External Defects   53
Metric   57
Variable Data   58
Attribute Data   60
Creating the Metric   63

Chapter 5   Step 2: Define the Improvement Teams 68
Identifying the Required Teams   68
Pareto Diagram   69
Staffing the Teams   73
Determining Required Skills and Knowledge   78
Roles and Responsibilities   78
Rules of Conduct   82
Notes   86

Chapter 6   Step 3: Identify Potential Causes   87
Flowcharting   87
Brainstorming   99
Fishbone Diagram   103
Prioritizing   105

**Chapter 7   Step 4: Investigation and Root
   Cause Identification**   108
Action Plan   108
Check Sheet   112
Stratification   122
Histogram   126
Scatter Diagram   130

Chapter 8   Step 5: Make Improvement Permanent   138

Institutionalization   138

Work Method Change   142

Physical Change   142

Procedural Change   145

Training   145

Notes   148

**Chapter 9   Step 6: Demonstrate Improvement
and Celebrate**   149

Back to Focused Metric   149

Success of the Enterprise   151

Team Recognition   153

SECTION THREE: GETTING STARTED   157

Chapter 10   Start Your Journey   159

Do Something   159

The Fallacy of Zero Defects   160

First Steps   163

Before and After   169

Chapter 11   Managing Change   170

Overview   170

Leadership   172

Participation   172

Training   175

A Six Sigma Change Management Model   175

Your Six Sigma Journey   181

Notes   181

Index   *183*

PREFACE

I was one of the original divisional quality directors at Motorola chartered with developing, training, and deploying the culture and methods of Six Sigma. We were able to reduce costs, improve efficiencies, and maximize customer satisfaction in all operations. Within the manufacturing operations, we reduced the cost of sales by 30 percent. In administrative and service functions, we reduced cycle times and cost by as much as 90 percent. In 1990 and 1991 our division was used as the internal benchmark for service and administrative quality.

This success was based on creating a Six Sigma culture in which goals and objectives were clearly defined and communicated, the creation of a six-step continuous improvement model utilizing the JUSE (Japanese Union of Scientists and Engineers) seven problem-solving tools, and the effective management of the change. This book is written so that others can learn and apply these techniques.

This book consists of three sections. Section One is about how to identify the need for a Six Sigma program and how to establish a Six Sigma culture. Section Two teaches a pragmatic six-step continuous improvement model. This continuous improvement model can be learned and used by all employees in manufacturing, administration, and service operations. Section Three presents methods for managing the change and a guide on what to expect during the phases of implementation.

Benefits to the Reader

❑ How to establish a Six Sigma culture
❑ A simple and practical continuous improvement model
❑ How to manage the change required for Six Sigma

This book is beneficial to all who are interested in improving their performance and the performance of the enterprise for which they work.

The first section will be most helpful to managers and leaders—those who must define and create the Six Sigma–based culture that will nurture a successful Six Sigma program. A Six Sigma culture starts with a clear understanding of who the customers are and what is required for complete customer satisfaction. Data systems must be established to measure and monitor customer satisfaction. Improvement goals must be set, and programs must be initiated to achieve the goals. Everyone must know their role in achieving complete customer satisfaction and success for the enterprise.

Key Elements of Six Sigma

❑ Focused on Customer Satisfaction
❑ Data
❑ Reach-Out Goals
❑ Team Based
❑ All Employees Involved
❑ Clear Definition and Understanding of Roles
❑ Personal Growth

The second section of the book is helpful to all employees. This section is about how to establish improvement programs that are customer focused, team based, and deployed throughout the entire workforce. The six-step continuous improvement method is equally applicable to manufacturing operations, administrative functions, and service organizations. The program must be focused on the key success initiatives of the company, which in turn are focused on complete customer satisfaction in all aspects of doing business. For some operations the customers will be external to the company, and for others the customers will be internal to the company. The tools and techniques presented in this book are applicable in all cases.

In the second section the reader will learn the JUSE seven tools of problem solving and how to apply these tools in a six-step process for continuous improvement to achieve Six Sigma performance levels.

JUSE Seven Tools

- ❑ Pareto Diagram
- ❑ Fishbone Diagram
- ❑ Check Sheet
- ❑ Histogram
- ❑ Stratification
- ❑ Scatter Diagram
- ❑ Charting

Section Three offers suggestions on how to start your Six Sigma initiatives and how to manage the changes that will occur.

Think continuous improvement. Without it, you are losing ground. Without it, the best case is that you are holding steady while your competitors are leaving you behind. The more likely case is that your performance is deteriorating while your competitors are improving. Systems left on their own tend to atrophy. As the world has evolved to a global market, competition has intensified. Superior product and service will distinguish the winners from the losers.

Six Sigma and the continuous improvement model are about tools and techniques that can be learned and successfully used by all employees. I have trained, facilitated, and coached this system to a very diverse group of enterprises. I use the term "enterprise" in the generic sense to include companies, operations within companies, small work groups, nonprofit organizations, retail operations, food service, financial services, and sales. Any group of people that is performing a service or creating a product will benefit from this.

Six Sigma is about total employee involvement. Many programs labeled Six Sigma include just a small portion of the company's total workforce. This results in getting very limited benefit while most of your resources, and the intelligence they possess, remain unused. The beauty of Six Sigma and the very core of its early development and successful application was that it included all employees. The major benefits of improved customer satisfaction, market share gains, reduced operating costs, profit improvements, and increased stock prices are fueled primarily by teams of direct labor employees. The material presented is useful to everyone within the enterprise from the senior executives, who will be setting the vision and supporting the programs, to the shop floor or office cubicle people who are performing the tasks.

Every enterprise exists to support a customer base. Customers are the only source of income or funding. Satisfying the customers beyond their expectations and better than your competition must be closely tied to the survival of every enterprise.

Six Sigma is about building quality into all of your operations. The quality levels required today cannot be achieved by inspecting quality in or by sorting good from bad at final outgoing. The service industry never has had the luxury of inspecting quality in. Every encounter in service is a moment of truth where customer expectations are either met or not. I refer to inspecting quality in as a luxury because even if you could do it, your costs of manufacturing would then be too high.

Six Sigma is about engaging the people who perform the work to determine why performance levels are not as good as they should be and to create the policies, procedures, and work practices that will ensure complete customer satisfaction. The benefits of having the workers develop their own solutions include a sense of ownership and pride. This also enables employees to utilize their innate intelligence and existing skills sets, to learn new skills, and to feel better about themselves and their roles in the success of the company. High morale is a natural result of using these methods.

The following quote is taken from one of Motorola's early Six Sigma teams. It is an excellent example of how people thought about this program and the results that they achieved. The members of this team were all direct labor employees from the factory floor.

There's a difference between interest *and* commitment. *When you're* interested *in doing something, you do it only when it's convenient. When you're* committed *to something, you accept no excuses, only results.*

The Basics of Six Sigma

How to create a culture that thinks and operates in terms of complete customer satisfaction. How to build a workforce that is engaged and committed to the success of the company.

1 August 1965

0115 GMT   North Atlantic off the coast of Norway. Depth 200 feet. Speed six knots. Heading 010. At the height of the Cold War, the American submarine *Sam Houston* is on patrol carrying sixteen nuclear missiles with multiple warheads. Its role is as a determent to Russia initiating a first-strike attack. The *Sam Houston,* and submarines like her, has the ability to retaliate with mass destruction.

0117 GMT   Loud noise and escaping steam in the engine room. Throughout the ship power is lost to lighting and operating systems. The machinist mates report that the main valve to the starboard electrical generator has failed. The chief of the watch reports that the valve has been isolated and the steam leak has stopped. The starboard generator is out of service. Forward, the auxiliary electrician has turned off power to all unnecessary loads. To keep the nuclear reactor temperature and pressure in the safe area, the operator has been adjusting control rod heights and pump speeds. The conning officer has ordered a depth change from 200 feet to 100 feet.

0118 GMT   "Conn, this is engineering. We have lost the starboard generator. Damage has been isolated. Damage assessment now in progress."
"Conn, this is the captain. What's the situation?"
"Engineering reports loss of starboard generator and is assessing damage."

0119 GMT   (Over the loudspeaker system): "This is the captain. We have lost half of our electrical generation capability. Rig ship for reduced power." The cook turns off all ovens and stovetops. All lights in crew's quarters are turned off. In the torpedo room, lighting is reduced to a few emergency lights. Coffeepots are killed. The missile technicians have activated emergency backup power.

0122 GMT   Machinist mate reports that the main steam valve to the starboard generator blew its packing. Stores has been contacted and is searching for spare parts.

0124 GMT   Stores reports that they have all necessary spare parts on board. They have been collected and are now being delivered to engineering. "Conn, this is engineering. Repair parts are on their way. Machinist mates estimate repair time to be six hours."

0125 GMT   "Captain, this is the Conn. Engineering reports that repair parts are in hand and estimate repair time of six hours."
"Okay Conn, I'm on my way up."

0130 GMT   From the Conn: "This is the captain. Congratulations to everyone for a job well done. All critical and necessary systems are operational. We will remain on reduced power for approximately six hours. That means we'll be having a cold breakfast this morning. Also, the smoking lamp is out until further notice. We've all been through these things before, and we'll all be inconvenienced together."

Yes, I was in the submarine service during the Cold War, and yes, I am proud of my service. But why would I start a book on Six Sigma based on this experience? Because operations like this are where a successful Six Sigma culture starts. What is notable about a submarine crew is that it is made up of diverse people with a variety of training and skills. All are well trained and qualified for their respective assignments. All realize that they are part of a larger whole with an important part to play in the successful completion of a mission. Although there is a hierarchy of command and responsibilities, everyone has respect for each member of the crew. Most importantly they realize that they will succeed or fail as a unit. Either the mission will be accomplished successfully and all hands will return safely to port and loved ones, or none of them will. During the Cold War two American submarines sank; there were no survivors.

Now, shift this to your work situation. Is there a hierarchy of command and responsibility? Is the workforce diverse, with different levels of education, training, and knowledge? Is everyone well trained and qualified for their respective assignments? The answer to these three questions is most likely yes. However, if documentation of the training needs and job certification requirements for a qualified employee at all job assignments is lacking, you must define them and commence remedial action to bring the incumbent workforce up to minimal requirements.

Do all of the employees realize that they are part of a larger whole? Do the employees realize what their roles are and how they contribute to the success of the company? Does everyone have respect for each member of the workforce? Is there a sense among all employees that they will succeed or fail as a unit? Unless you have already established a Six Sigma, or equivalent, culture, the answer to these questions is probably no.

Six Sigma is about creating a culture where all of these things are established and deployed throughout the entire workforce. It is about providing a structure in which everyone knows what is expected of them, what their contributions are, and how to measure their own success. It is about creating an environment where people feel good about themselves. It is about providing the training and tools that everyone will need to maximize their and their team's performance. It is about being results oriented, fueled by continuous improvement, and focused on customer satisfaction.

A Six Sigma culture contains:

- ❑ A diverse workforce with varying levels of education
- ❑ Training programs to teach the required skills
- ❑ An understanding by everyone of their roles for success
- ❑ A unified workforce where everyone feels like part of a greater whole
- ❑ Mutual respect for everyone's knowledge and skills
- ❑ A commitment to succeed
- ❑ A focus on customer satisfaction

CHAPTER 1

The Grass Roots of Six Sigma

Why It Had to Be Invented

In the mid–1980s Motorola was losing ground in every market that they served. Customer dissatisfaction and frustration with Motorola were epidemic. Operating costs were too high, which led to dismal profits. In all cases the lost market share was being taken over by Japanese competitors. I remember Bob Galvin, Motorola's CEO from 1970 to 1988 and chairman of the board from 1964 to 1990, saying that if the Japanese had not existed, we would have needed to invent them. I interpreted this to mean that someone had to give us a wake-up call.

Throughout its customer base, Motorola had a reputation for being arrogant. Bob Galvin was chagrined by an article in one of the trade magazines, in which the head of purchasing of one of our major customers for communications equipment was quoted as saying about Motorola,

"Love, love, love the product; hate, hate, hate the company." Bob cited this quote several times to his leadership team.

Motorola's systems for doing business were not designed for customer satisfaction. Contract reviews, responses to requests for quote, invoicing, responses to customer complaints, and most other administrative and service operations were victims of a system that allowed for apathetic management and disinterested workers. The internal bureaucracy fed on itself with little regard for serving the customers. Response times were long, and responses usually were not designed to satisfy the customer.

The quality and reliability of Motorola's product were also not what they should have been. Customers were receiving too many out-of-box failures. After the product passed their incoming requirements, they often suffered high levels of early-life failures. Warranty returns were a major drain on profits. A wireless communications division was suffering huge losses, threatened lawsuits, and lost business with a major customer. The division quality manager was tasked with determining what was causing such poor field performance. His study of early-life failures discovered that they were predominately units that had failed at final test and had to go back through a rework cycle.

Fortunately, the same Japanese that were destroying Motorola in the marketplace also provided a benchmark for how things could be done better. A group of senior managers and executives were sent on a benchmarking tour of Japan to study operating methods and product quality levels. They discovered that Japan had a national program for employee involvement and teaming, focused on improving operations to better serve the customers. The Japanese had managed to use not only the muscle that their employees provided but also their brains and knowledge. They also discovered, no surprise here, that the more complicated a product, the higher the opportunities for failure.

Motorola's problems were present in all of their business units and product lines. Something had to happen, and it had to be major, and it had to get positive results quickly. Thus was born the need to create Six Sigma.

The Birth of Six Sigma

From its customers Motorola learned that they needed to change their systems in all operations—manufacturing, service, administration, and sales—to focus on total customer satisfaction. From the Japanese they learned that including all of your employees in the company brain trust was an effective means of increasing efficiency and morale. From the Japanese they also learned that simpler designs result in higher levels of quality and reliability. From the early-life field failure study they learned that they needed to improve manufacturing techniques to ensure that products were built right the first time.

Motorola's leaders pulled this together to establish the vision and set the framework for Six Sigma. Posters were hung up, and small cards were given to all employees (see Figure 1-1).

Thus was Six Sigma launched in 1987. The corporate leaders toured the world to all Motorola sites to explain that this new initiative is going to be the operating mantra of Motorola for the future. Bob Galvin personally traveled

---

OUR FUNDAMENTAL OBJECTIVE

(Everyone's Overriding Responsibility)

Total Customer Satisfaction

KEY BELIEFS—*how we will always act*
* Constant Respect for People
* Uncompromising Integrity

KEY GOALS—*what we must accomplish*
* Best in Class
  -*People*
  -*Marketing*
  -*Technology*
  -*Product: Software, Hardware and Systems*
  -*Manufacturing*
  -*Service*

KEY INITIATIVES—*how we will do it*
* Six Sigma Quality
* Total Cycle Time Reduction
* Product, Manufacturing and Environmental
  Leadership
* Profit Improvement
* Empowerment for All, in a Participative,
  Cooperative and Creative Workplace

Figure 1-1. Motorola launch.

to most major sites worldwide. Of course, there was a lot of skepticism. This looked like another program du jour. "We'll get excited about it, and two months from now nobody will remember" was typical of the statements you heard at all levels.

However, the corporate leaders did a very thorough job

of deploying Six Sigma throughout Motorola around the globe. They asked for Six Sigma reports, and they expected quality levels to be the first agenda item at all operational reviews. Soon it became the modus operandi throughout Motorola.

A key figure in all of this was Bill Smith. Bill was a high-level quality leader who is credited with developing the mathematics of Six Sigma. The arithmetic of Six Sigma was created as a way of leveling the playing field throughout Motorola. The concept of opportunities-for-error was developed to account for differing complexities. An *opportunity-for-error* is something that must be performed correctly in order to deliver conforming product or service. A product that took forty process steps to complete is obviously more difficult to build than a product requiring two process steps. Likewise, an invoice consisting of forty line items is more difficult to complete error free than an invoice containing two line items. To adjust for the differences in determining the numbers of opportunities for error among assembly manufacturing, process manufacturing, administrative tasks, and services operations, formulas used were developed empirically. Thus, a manufacturing operation in Malaysia could be fairly compared to an order-entry work unit in Plantation, Florida. This was very important within Motorola and was a key to its success at Motorola.

Sigma calculations are controversial. The premises of processing attribute data (data that is discrete, such as good or bad, win or loss, conforming or nonconforming) using the normal curve and z-table associated with variables data (data that is continuous and centered around a target value with natural variation from the target) violate many of the rules of statistics. The empirical formulas used to calculate opportunities for error have the potential for overstating the complexity of an operation, which in turn would lead to a deflated defect rate. Finally, the premise of accounting for variation over time by adding 1.5 sigma to the actual z-table sigma level looks fishy to many first-time observers. During the early days of spreading Six Sigma to companies other than Motorola, I made many presentations at conventions, conferences, company-specific executive breakout sessions, and suppliers to Motorola. At most of these the validity of the sigma value calculation was challenged.

Peter Pande et al. state in *The Six Sigma Way*, "Overall, you should think of Sigma-scale measures as an optional element of the Six Sigma system. We know of quite a few businesses—including some units of GE—that express their overall measures as [a defect rate] and only occasionally translate them to the Sigma scale."[1] I agree with this. Since I left Motorola, many of the Six Sigma–based systems that I have developed do not use a Sigma-value calculation. It was important for Motorola and worked well for them; however, you can achieve the same results by driving for continuous improvement on any scale.

Bill Smith was far more than the developer of the Six Sigma algorithms. He was the heart and soul of its deployment throughout Motorola and was often referred to as the father of Six Sigma. He had a deep understanding of the contributions that the front-line workers made to Motorola's success. He was just as comfortable with the dignitaries in Washington as he was coaching a group of direct labor participants. I had the honor of working with him and being mentored by him for two years. Unfortunately, he died suddenly and prematurely from a massive stroke. I can't help but wonder where Six Sigma would be today if he had lived. Perhaps his greatest attribute was his pragmatism.

In *Total Quality Control,* Armand Feigenbaum defines "total quality management" (TQM) as follows:

> *A quality system is the agreed on, companywide and plantwide operating work structure, documented in effective, integrated technical and managerial procedures, for guiding the coordinated actions of the people, the machines, and the information of the company and plant in the best and most practical ways to assure customer quality satisfaction and economical costs of quality.*[2]

In 1989 Bill Smith defined Six Sigma as:

> *Organized common sense.*

Black Belts and Green Belts

Within the high-tech manufacturing operations within Motorola, the practice of training some engineers and technologists in advanced forms of experimental design, data analysis, and process control was initiated in the early 1980s—prior to the introduction of Six Sigma. These individuals were known as local statistical resources (LSR). Usually, they came from the process engineering or manufacturing engineering groups. I was on the leading edge of these initiatives at Motorola. Typically, one out of ten engineers was trained as statistic resources for the engineering and technical community. These individuals are now referred to as black belts.

During this same time, factory workers were formed into teams based on the Japanese model of quality circles. These team members received some training and coaching in problem-solving methods and in the interpersonal behaviors expected of team members. As an engineering manager, I was a trainer, coach, and facilitator of these teams. As the improvement efforts within Motorola evolved, and following the introduction of Six Sigma, these teams evolved into the total customer satisfaction, or TCS, teams. Team members were trained on problem-solving tools, continuous improvement models, and teaming skills. These individuals were the precursors of green belts.

The terms "black belt" and "green belt" were not applied to the Six Sigma program at Motorola until the 1990s. Since that time, as Six Sigma has grown to become recognized as a leading-edge standard for companies in manufacturing, service, and retail, many programs include special-assignment employees with the title of black belt or green belt. All too often, these individuals are external to the operations that they support, which is a very expensive and less-than-optimum structure for instilling Six Sigma. There is a high probability that such an approach will disenfranchise most employees and give them a convenient avenue for abdicating their responsibilities. Short-term benefits can be realized, but the long-term cultural way of thinking about customer satisfaction and continuous improvement will not be infused throughout the greater workforce.

A highly effective and cost-beneficial method for deploying green-belt and black-belt skills throughout an enterprise is to not create specialists with the title of black belt and green belt, but rather to consider all of your employees as potential green belts. All employees are capable of learning the skills and techniques required to become a green belt. From this "army" of green belts, select those individuals who will receive the additional training required to become your black belts. Your first-line supervisors and middle management associates are ideal candidates; however, you will discover that some front-line workers also exhibit the aptitude for becoming black belts. These individuals who have an aptitude for facilitating and leading teams will require additional training in influence management skills, coaching, teaming techniques, program management, and running effective meetings. Typically, 5 to 10 percent of the employees will be needed as black belts.

In high-tech operations, a small number of individuals trained in advanced statistical analysis and experimental design will be needed. These individuals can also be called black belts.

The goal of any enterprise should be to get all of its employees trained in the techniques required to become a green belt, including the seven problem-solving tools, the six-step model for continuous improvement, and the interpersonal skills required to effectively participate on a team. All of these techniques are described in Section Two of this book.

One of the lessons learned at Motorola was that the direct labor teams drove the majority of the cost savings, quality improvements, and higher customer satisfaction levels. The people who actually perform the tasks are the experts on the task. They have a sense of what is preventing them from doing a better job, and by utilizing the six-step continuous improvement method, they can come up with the solutions. Also, when the workers take on responsibility for their own performance, there is a sense of ownership and accountability. When they determine the fixes and the changes that are necessary for improving their operation, buy-in is a given. This pride of ownership and improved performance leads to greater worker efficiency and high morale.

According to Joyce Wycoff:

> *When an organization commits to creating an environment which stimulates the growth of everyone in the organization, amazing things start to happen: ideas pop up everywhere, people start to work together instead of "playing politics"; new opportunities appear; customers begin to notice service and attitude improvements; collections of individuals begin to coalesce into teams."*[3]

I have been involved in many successful programs. As employees become more experienced and effective with Six Sigma tools and the results come rolling in, something magical happens. There comes a point in time when you walk into the work area and you can feel the human energy, like static electricity, in the air. Those of you who have had similar experiences know what I am talking about. I hope that you who have not yet had this thrill will soon experience it.

By infusing black belt and green belt skills throughout the entire incumbent workforce, you are developing the individuals who will create your Six Sigma culture. Everyone will learn new skills and new ways of thinking about how to optimize their performance. *And*, you will avoid the long-term added expense of creating and funding special-assignment job functions. *And*, you will be creating an atmosphere of high morale, where all employees feel good about themselves and their contributions to the success of the enterprise.

The Required Components

The chart in Figure 1-2 is from the first Six Sigma briefing used to teach companies beyond Motorola what the six key ingredients are for transforming from business as usual to a Six Sigma culture. Chapter 2 contains more on how to create this culture.

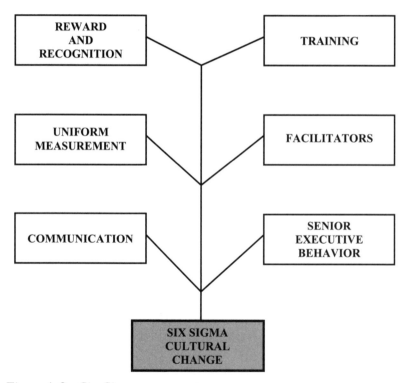

Figure 1-2. Six Sigma components.

The six components are:

Reward and Recognition is a system for celebrating the accomplishments of a team or work unit, including a way to be honored in front of the workforce. Executive bonuses must be tied to the success of the Six Sigma program.

Training must be provided to teach everyone the new skills and knowledge required to implement Six Sigma.

Uniform Measurement requires that all work units in manufacturing, administration, and service determine what is acceptable delivery to the customers. Unacceptable deliveries are counted and converted to a defect rate measurement.

Facilitators are the employees who have the aptitude and receive the training required to work with others and assist them in the transition to Six Sigma.

Communication must be provided so that everyone understands what is expected of them.

Senior Executive Behavior must model the expectations of Six Sigma.

Notes

1. Peter S. Pande, Robert T. Neuman, and Roland R. Cavanagh, *The Six Sigma Way* (New York: McGraw-Hill, 2000).

2. Armand V. Feigenbaum, *Total Quality Control,* 3rd edition (New York: McGraw-Hill, 1951), p. 14.

3. Joyce Wycoff, *Transformation Thinking* (New York: Berkley, 1995), p. 14.

CHAPTER 2

Creating the Cultural Structure

Senior Management Roles and Engagement

Six Sigma is a successful evolution of total quality management systems. Because total quality management or Six Sigma provides a system for how you will run your enterprise, it could just as appropriately be called "total business management" or "total operational management." We probably have W. Edwards Deming and Joseph M. Juran to thank for these programs being identified under the quality banner. Their groundbreaking programs and the results they achieved in Japan led to American management "rediscovering" them in the early 1980s.

This birth of their popularity was fueled by the dismal business performance of American companies competing with Japan, the same malady that prompted Motorola to create Six Sigma. The essence of Deming's teachings and Six Sigma is that they bring together operating systems and processes (either manufacturing, administrative, or service) with a high degree of respect for the workers asked to perform within these processes, optimizing this combination for serving the customer.

Of course, the answers were always there. American management just wasn't listening.

A good way to understand a Six Sigma–based total quality management system is by defining the words in terms of:

TOTAL	Everyone committed
QUALITY	Meeting the customers' expectations
MANAGEMENT	Collaborative focus

Stated another way: *Within a Six Sigma system, everyone is committed to meeting the customers' expectations through the use of a collaborative focus.*

Effective Six Sigma systems have many things in common. Employees at all levels within all operations, administrative departments, and service organizations know their quality levels and are committed to making them better. Everyone shares a common passion for success. Operating policies and procedures are driven by customer satisfaction. Customers like doing business with the company. There is an atmosphere of high morale. Processes are repeatable and under control; the outcome is predictable. This applies to administrative and service functions as well as to manufacturing outputs. Product and service outputs, both internal and external, are verified to meet customers' needs.

Benchmarks for companies that have effective systems in place are the winners of the Malcolm Baldrige National

Quality Award. A study of the winning companies from the first years of that award showed that they all had many aspects of Six Sigma in place.

Commonalities of Malcolm Baldrige National Quality Award recipients are:

1. All operations and functions concentrate on total customer satisfaction. This applies whether serving internal or external customers.

2. There are mechanisms in place to determine customer satisfaction levels. Customer satisfaction is constantly monitored, and programs are in place to improve it.

3. The Quality Culture is cascaded down from the senior management leadership team. They have defined the corporate vision and have deployed it throughout the company.

4. Senior management is involved with monitoring, mentoring, and encouraging the new culture. They constantly reinforce positive performance.

5. Supplier relations have changed from simply buying based on price alone to buying from the lowest-cost-to-do-business-with suppliers. Suppliers are expected to have systems in place to ensure delivery of defect-free parts or service on time.

6. The role of middle management is changed. Middle management is often the most threatened group of employees. At the same time, they are often the group expected to be most instrumental in facilitating and driving cultural changes.

7. There are internal controls in place to identify defects and mistakes. There are active programs to eliminate errors.

8. Benchmarking is used as a tool to drive improvement of the company in all aspects of doing business.

9. There is some form of employee empowerment. Or, at least, there is a system that allows and encourages employees to use their intelligence and take the initiative required to make things better.

10. There are metrics in place to measure the quality levels of all operations and functions. Attached to these are programs for continuous improvement.

11. Training, training, training. As employees are asked to assume new roles, to redefine what makes them successful, to learn new skills, and to learn the new cultural norms, training is imperative.

12. There are aggressive goals. People are challenged to work more efficiently. They are taught the skills and techniques required to achieve higher levels of performance.

13. Teams are abundant. In some cases there are cross-functional and multilevel teams. At the very minimum, work units are identified as teams and are taught the interpersonal skills required to function as a team. Supervisors transition from the traditional command-and-control role to the role of coach-mentor-facilitator.

14. There is a reward and recognition system in place. As new behaviors are expected from everyone, positive examples are recognized and celebrated.

First and foremost, senior management must determine and create the culture that will enable all of these things to happen. They must set the vision for the enterprise. For example, in *Alice's Adventures in Wonderland,* when Alice meets the Cheshire Cat at a fork in the road, she asks the Cat,

"Would you tell me, please, which way I ought to go from here?" "That depends a good deal on where you want to get to," said the Cat. "I don't much care where——" said Alice. "Then it doesn't matter which way you go," said the Cat.[1] Without a clearly defined and communicated vision and key measures for success, your employees will be like poor Alice, lost in a wonderland of strange creatures and mad behavior.

Senior management must be resolved to do whatever it takes to make the new culture work. They must be willing and able to modify their own behaviors to model the new rules and norms. They must be committed to the long haul. The course must be set and held steady. It took the Japanese twenty years to realize the benefits of their quality programs. Under the tutelage of Deming and others, the Japanese started these quality programs in the early 1950s. It wasn't until the 1970s that the Japanese became a major market-share holder in the United States.

Organizational Development

A key to the success of Six Sigma is that everyone in the company must know what they contribute to the success of the company. Everyone must have a clear understanding of why they are employed and receiving a paycheck. They must understand this in light of how their actions affect the customers. Recently on a trip through the Midwest, I was listening to National Public Radio. The host of the show, who was interviewing local farmers, asked one farmer what he did. He answered that he fed the world. He could have said any number of things such as plow fields, repair tractors, or grow vegetables. But this man understood his value-add contribution. This may be somewhat more difficult within a large corporation, yet it is even more important.

The leadership of the company must complete an articulate framework of how the company will function to serve its customer base. One easy model for an Organizational Development framework is the acronym MOST, which represents Mission, Objectives, Strategies, and Tactics.

Mission

The company must make a clear and concise statement of why it exists and the customers that it serves. The mission statement may also include how the company serves the customers' customers. A good mission statement must contain a description of what success will look like when you are fulfilling it.

A mission statement is more concrete than a *vision* statement. Whereas the vision has an ethereal quality, the mission statement must be reach-out yet achievable. A vision has a sense of "In my next life I want to be. . . ." A typical vision may read, "To be recognized by everyone worldwide as the best company to work for." It is doubtful that three people living on the same block could agree on the criteria for the best company to work for let alone the entire population of the earth.

A *mission* statement may read, "To be the market leader for headlights sold to American automakers." Unless you are already the market leader, this is an aggressive goal. It can be measured, and you can ascertain when you are fulfilling it. It also contains why the company exists—to build and sell headlights—and the customers it serves—American automakers.

Objectives

Objectives are the quantifiable high-level goals of the company. They are the statements of how you will determine and measure your success. They must be statements of what you are striving to achieve; however, the numerical targets should not be published. Competitors can gain damaging insight into your business health, and customers will often use this information to negotiate price reductions. The company should hold the actual performance to objectives in tight security.

Objectives might look like this:

Increase market share

Reduce manufacturing costs

Increase new product introductions

Reduce cycle times for product delivery and service response

Zero safety incidents

Reduce water and air emissions

Improve profit

Improve quality in product, service, and administrative functions

The number of objectives should be between five and eight. If the list is too large, it becomes a laundry list of wishes. If the list is too small, it can be limiting. You want to provide a concise list around which all organizations can focus their actions and priorities.

Strategies

Strategies are the means that you will use to accomplish the objectives. Strategies define the expectations of your culture. From these strategies your employees should have a clear understanding of what is expected behavior.

Strategy statements may include:

- ❑ Respect for all people
- ❑ Cross-functional teaming
- ❑ Continuous improvement programs
- ❑ Superior services to our community, customers, and employees
- ❑ State-of-the-art technology
- ❑ Open communication between employees at all levels
- ❑ Training and personal growth for all employees
- ❑ Innovative manufacturing techniques
- ❑ High integrity
- ❑ A clean and safe work environment
- ❑ Exceeding customers' expectations in all aspects of doing business with us

The mission statement, objectives, and strategies are typically generated by the senior management team at an off-site location. A two-day session facilitated by an organizational development facilitator is an effective means to accomplish this. Mission, objectives, and strategies must come from the company leadership team. These are a top-down communication of what is to be accomplished, how success will be determined, and what means are to be used.

Tactics

Tactics are the actions that will be taken, within the strategy guidelines, to accomplish the objectives and fulfill the company's mission. Once the mission, objectives, and strategies have been communicated throughout the company, each department and division must provide a detailed action plan containing:

What will be done

Who is responsible for doing it

When it will be completed

These action plans form the foundation for what each work unit is expected to get done daily, weekly, and monthly throughout the year. These plans need to be tied to at least one of the company objectives. In this way, every employee throughout the company will have a clear understanding of what is expected of them, what their value to the overall success of the company is, and why they are employed.

A good action plan is posted and distributed to all affected employees. Work units must review their performance and progress on a regular time interval. Depending on the volume and cycle time of work, work units should review their performance weekly, biweekly, or monthly. Division or department heads should review each work unit at least once a month. This gives an opportunity to provide feedback and to identify where barriers may need to be removed, what resources need to be added, and where management may need to spend more time assisting their subordinates. Regular formal reviews also continue to reinforce the concept that we are in this together.

Requirements for Change

In the late 1980s, Motorola received many requests from conference organizers and individual companies for a briefing on what was entailed in establishing a Six Sigma culture, on how the mathematics worked for determining a Sigma level, and on the tools and techniques that led to the company's success. In those briefings we initially presented the "Required Components" fishbone diagram (see Figure 1-2 in Chapter 1), expanding on each of the six components required for a Six Sigma cultural change. We also spent a lot of time on how to measure defects and on the mathematics of how to convert a defect rate into a Sigma value.

By the early 1990s, these companies realized that a transition to Six Sigma would require changes and that they would need to manage the change. We then began getting questions about how we had managed this complex change. In response, we developed the chart shown in Figure 2-1, and used it in some of these briefings. The elements of that chart are explained as follows:

❑ *Vision*. Vision is established by creating the vision statement that sets the framework for the mission, objectives, and strategies. All of this provides everyone with a clear view of what is to be accomplished and how it is to be accomplished. It is recommended that each division, department, and work unit create their own mission statement to indicate their role in fulfilling the company's mission and their contributions toward accomplishing the objectives. This will ensure that they understand the vision as defined and communicated by senior management.

❑ *Skills*. Skills are instilled through training. Training is perhaps the most important aspect of managing change. People need to be taught the language, expectations, and rules of the new culture. Technologists and engineers need to be taught experimental designs and process control techniques. Everyone needs to learn basic problem-solving

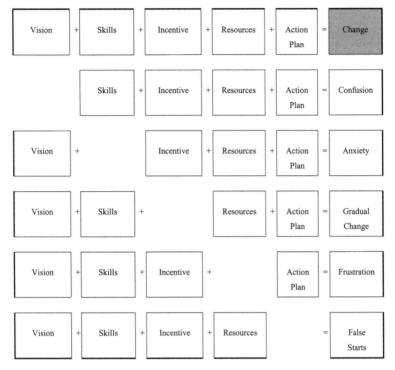

Figure 2-1. Managing complex change.

tools and a logical model for how to apply them to continuously improve performance. Everyone must learn teaming and interpersonal skills. Managers at all levels need to be taught leadership skills—how to transition from control management to facilitating leadership.

❑ *Incentive.* Incentive is instilled in senior management by tying bonuses to the objectives and creating the new culture within their infrastructures. Within senior management incentive plans, a minimum of 30 percent of their bonus potential should be dependent on achieving quality goals. For everyone within the middle ranks, pay raises can be attached to how well their work units complete action plans and meet their goals.

Incentive for work unit members is accomplished through a reward and recognition system. The system should not include monetary rewards. At Motorola we learned this lesson. It was virtually impossible to create a monetary reward system that was equitable. For every employee who was motivated by receiving a bonus, at least ten employees who didn't receive a bonus were demotivated.

We did have great success with small rewards, such as key chains, pins for your badge, two movie tickets, coffee cups, and other similar items. The most effective means to motivate workers was through recognition. Individuals and teams were highlighted at monthly communication meetings. Senior and middle managers would have an informal coffee break with a team to discuss how things were going and offer helpful suggestions. Teams that accomplished a significant milestone were treated to lunch.

❑ *Resources*. Resources required to establish teams are minimal. Members of continuous improvement teams need to be provided one hour a week for team meetings and an additional hour to work on team-specific projects. When first confronted with losing their workers for two hours each week, most managers are concerned about productivity. In fact, in all cases that I was involved with, productivity actually went up. One manufacturing group that had 90 percent participation on teams actually saw a 30 percent increase in productivity. An analysis showed that some gains were attributable to improvements identified and implemented by the teams. However, the greatest gains were achieved because people were working more efficiently and were making better use of their discretionary time.

Resources include expert help. In the early stages you will require consultants, either internal or external, to assist the teams with start-up. People will need to be trained. Teams will need to be facilitated. Managers will need to be coached.

❑ *Action Plans.* Action plans are part of the organizational development plan. Divisions, departments, and work units are required to generate action plans. As part of their continuous improvement programs, teams are required to issue action plans. Once these action plans are created, they must be worked and completed to schedule.

Action plans are "living documents." This means that as actions are completed, they are removed from the action plan and archived. As new information is attained, new action items need to be added. The operational structure must provide for weekly and monthly reviews on how well each entity is doing on completing their action items on schedule and achieving the desired results.

The elements of a Six Sigma culture are:

❑ Active and visible senior management involvement
❑ A mission statement defining success
❑ Objectives and strategies
❑ Action plans detailing tactics
❑ A methodology for managing change
❑ Training
❑ Teams

Note

1. Lewis Carroll, *Alice's Adventures in Wonderland & Through the Looking-Glass* (New York: Bantam, 1981), p. 46.

σ

CHAPTER 3

Preliminary Tasks

What Do You Want?

Before you embark on a major campaign to improve your company and the skill levels of your employees, you need to ask what it is that you are trying to accomplish and what is required to get you there. If you want to be a cowboy or cowgirl when you grow up, then you should learn how to ride a horse and have someone teach you gun safety. On the other hand, if you want to be a firefighter, start taking lifesaving classes and learn the science of extinguishing fires. This may sound silly, but if any program that you decide to initiate is going to work, you must be committed for a very long period of time. So, it is best to determine that this is really something that you want to do.

Meet with the senior management team, and decide what you want your culture to be. If you decide that you want a Six Sigma–based culture, you need to be aware of the essence of Six Sigma. A Six Sigma culture is one that focuses on the voice of the customer. Your decisions, programs, and operating systems will be geared to total customer satisfaction. Service, administration, and production operating systems will be designed with the belief that the customer is always right. Compensation and corrective actions for substandard product or unsatisfactory service will be done quickly and in the customers' favor. Customers asking for satisfaction will not have to hear "no" followed by the that's-not-our-policy mantra.

Six Sigma cultures include teaming and empowerment. When committing to a Six Sigma culture, you are committing to releasing a great deal of the historically centrally held information and power. Employees at all levels will have access to the information they need to make sound judgments, and they will be trusted to do so. Time will be made available during working hours for employees to meet and work on continuous improvement programs. The required training will be identified and funded. You need to determine and communicate the level of empowerment to which you are willing to go.

Before you launch a Six Sigma program, you need to complete your organizational development. Vision, mission, objectives, strategies, and tactical expectations all need to be documented and communicated. It is an excellent idea to complete a cross-functional mapping (see Chapter 6, Step 3). Identify what it is that you do now, the "As Is" situation. Then identify what you would like the system to look like to be a more efficient, user-friendly system, the "Should Be" situation. Then identify all of the actions that must take place to transition from the "As Is" to the "Should Be." Complete these actions with urgency.

Determine who will be your initial green belts and black belts. Chapter 1 listed some guidelines for the number of black belts. As the program grows, every employee within your company should be targeted to become a green belt. This is the best way to create an environment where everyone is a positive change agent. You need to identify the skill levels and training required to create your army of green belts and your cadre of black belts. Regardless of company size or markets served, green belts need to learn the tools, techniques, and model presented in Section Two. All enterprises require black belts with interpersonal, teaming, coaching, facilitation, and basic problem-solving skills. The type of business that you are in determines additional skills required by black belts. If your manufacturing operations are highly technical and controlled mainly by variable data, then you will need black belts that have been trained in experimental design and advanced process control techniques.

You need to identify where you are going to get the resources required to train and facilitate the establishment of your Six Sigma culture. Internal resources need to be identified and developed. External, experienced resources are required during the first year or two. The program should be designed so that external resources are utilized to develop the internal resources. As the internal resources are developed, the dependency on external resources should be phased out.

Selecting Projects

Start with your customer data. Typically, every company has file cabinets, or the electronic equivalent, full of historical complaints and returns from customers. It is also typical that very few companies use this data. The first step is to convert this data into information. Go through the data and determine the chronic reasons for the complaints. The useful tool to use here is a Pareto diagram. (See Chapter 5, Step 2 for a detailed description of Pareto diagrams.) This is an excellent way to prioritize your programs. Usually you will find three to six big reasons why your customers are unhappy with your product or service.

Once you know the reasons for customer dissatisfaction, determine what departments and work units are involved in providing the product and service. Identify the teams that will be needed to improve the performance, and recruit team members from every unit involved. Provide the required training. Charter the teams with eliminating errors and defects.

Another tool for gathering customer information is an annual customer satisfaction survey, best conducted by a third-party service provider experienced in interviewing customers. These surveys will yield information that otherwise will go unknown. Many customers will not complain, often because they do not like the confrontation associated with complaining. They quietly drift away to one of your competitors.

A third-party provider can offer anonymity and put customer representatives at ease. Experienced third-party providers also can digest the information and deliver a report with prioritized issues that you need to improve. An annual customer satisfaction survey contains both closed-ended questions and open-ended questions. A typical closed-ended question may be, "Compared to other suppliers, the timeliness and professionalism from Customer Service is: (excellent (good (average (fair (poor." Using 5 for excellent, 4 for good, 3 for average, 2 for fair, and 1 for poor, the numerical scores for each of the questions are summed. This provides the information necessary to prioritize customer satisfaction improvement projects.

A typical open-ended question may be, "What three things do you like least about doing business with XYZ?" The patterns and issues in the subjective information contained in the responses to such questions will provide additional information, leading to customer satisfaction improvement projects.

You also need to look at your financial performance. Determine where you are spending too much money due to poor quality. For example:

❑ How much of your cost-of-manufacturing is caused by rework and repair?

❑ How much of your cost-of-manufacturing is caused by in-process scrap?

❑ How much of your customer service budget is used for doing damage control following customer complaints?

❑ How much money are you spending on final inspections because you can't trust your operation to produce defect-free product?

❑ How much business have you lost because of poor service or product?

❑ How much could improved quality increase your market share?

Every line item on your balance sheet is affected, either positively or negatively, by your quality performance. Capture your costs of poor quality and prioritize the need for continuous improvement teams.

Collecting Data

Remember that within a Six Sigma culture, decisions are made and programs are established based on data. If you don't have the data that you need, establish some way to start collecting it. Keep files of why customers are complaining. If you lose a customer, follow up and get the real answer to why they went to one of your competitors.

You need data to identify where your problems are. You need data to establish a baseline of your historical performance. From this baseline, you need to set a goal of ten-fold improvement every two years. This is the Six Sigma rate of improvement standard. Then you need to monitor your performance against your goal. If you are meeting or exceeding your goal, stay the course. If you are not meeting your goal, regroup and redesign your programs.

Identifying Required Teams

You must take a cross-functional view of all parties involved in delivering product or service. If customers are chronically receiving product late, who is involved? It starts with sales receiving the order and communicating a realistic delivery date. Order entry personnel are responsible for getting it into production. Production control people are responsible for scheduling it properly. Production is responsible for operating a predictable factory flow. Factory engineering must design the factory layout and machine centers for optimum performance. Manufacturing Engineering must design processes that are controllable and predictable. Maintenance must keep equipment running. Warehousing must have a system that allows product to flow through quickly. Logistics must maintain an efficient delivery system.

So, if one of your prioritized programs is to improve customer on-time delivery, then you need to form a team that includes members from sales, order entry, production control, production, factory engineering, manufacturing engineering, maintenance, warehousing, and logistics.

If this team decides that none of them are at fault, that the real problem is the lousy product design that engineering gave them to build, then you need to add a representative from design engineering to the team. Any time a team starts using the term "them," someone from "them" needs to be added to the team.

Things that must be done prior to creating your Six Sigma program are:

- ❑ Determine what you want to accomplish
- ❑ Decide who will be black belts and green belts
- ❑ Define the training programs required for black-belt and green-belt candidates
- ❑ Select the initial projects targeted for improvement
- ❑ Establish the required data collection systems
- ❑ Identify the required teams

A Six Sigma Continuous Improvement Teaming Model

How to engage the entire workforce in the success of
an enterprise using customer-focused techniques and
quality-enhancing tools.

This section consists of a continuous improvement model and the tools of improvement arranged in a logical flow to get the desired results. The emphasis is on all employees. This model and the basic tools utilized can be learned and effectively applied by everyone. There are many statistically based programs that are helpful for driving improvements on very technical problems. These programs are good for what they are designed to do. The limitation is that often they only engage a small percentage of the workforce. Typically, a few managers and a few technologists or engineers will be involved. There are also some good problem-solving techniques available that, all too often, are applied only after a customer-upsetting incident has occurred.

The program presented in this section is designed with easy-to-learn tools that enable all employees to be involved in continuous improvement activities. This program is applicable to improving the performance in all work units within manufacturing, service, and retail operations.

According to Kauro Ishikawa, Executive Director, QC Circle Headquarters, Japan:

> *QC Circles [the early Japanese version of Continuous Improvement Teams] are usually introduced into production workshops. However, the Circle has already expanded beyond the production floor, for example, to offices, sales departments, warehouses, banks, insurance companies and so on. An increasing number of nonproduction QC Circles now present their cases at QC Conferences. Many people seem to think quality control deals only with quality of products and manufacturing operations in general. However, the QC Circle concept can be effectively introduced to any kind of work or service.*[1]

These tools and this method can be learned by all employees within a company. It is a very simple, yet powerful, method for giving all departments, work units, and individuals a chance to be part of the solutions. It is imperative that some up-front work is done in order to create the right culture where everyone knows his or her roles, responsibilities, accountability, and how success will be measured. I have been involved in companies where over 90 percent of the employees were team members applying the tools and techniques contained in this section. The most rewarding ancillary effect of these programs has been the high morale that they create. With a highly motivated workforce using the right tools, customers enjoy doing business with you and the financial results happen in a very positive way.

Another benefit to the methods contained in this section is that they are designed to be used proactively. You don't have to wait for an upset customer before identifying areas for improvement. Things can be good, and can still benefit from improvements—what can't? These tools and techniques can also be used on problem areas of chronic customer dissatisfaction. In such cases, the team will start with a problem, improve it to the point where it is fixed, and then continue on with any necessary improvements to make it the best-in-class benchmark for other companies to envy.

Also, this is customer based and customer focused. Often there is confusion on who the customer is. Customers can be either internal or external to a company. While it is easy to identify external customers, it is more difficult to identify internal customers. Every employee within an enterprise must have a clear understanding of why they are employed. Every employee in every enterprise must either be doing value-add work to sell, build, and deliver product or service to an external customer, or they must be supporting those individuals in the value-add chain.

As part of understanding roles and responsibilities, every work unit, and individuals within those work units, must go through a process of identifying what they do. What they do is their product, and for whom they do it is their customer. Also, to perform these do's, they have needs, and the providers of their needs are their suppliers. Each do/need pair is an interaction. Every Six Sigma process is a closed-loop system of interactions where customer satisfaction is understood, measured, and improved.

Some groundwork needs to be completed before embarking on continuous improvement projects within the Six Sigma program. Once an enterprise has initiated a Six Sigma program, work units and operations within the enterprise must complete some preliminary steps that ensure that the right things are being worked on. Continuous improvement projects must be properly prioritized such that the fruits of their labor will result in improved customer satisfaction. It is important that work units and operations view their activities as part of a larger system. They must think beyond the confines of what they do and think in terms of why they do the things that they do and on whom they are dependent. Before initiating a continuous improvement project, the responsible work unit or operation must complete the following steps:

1. Identify the product they create or the service they provide.
2. Identify their customer(s), and determine the customers' needs.
3. Identify their suppliers and what they need from the suppliers.

4. Define their process for doing the work.
5. Establish metrics for measuring the goodness of their process and feedback mechanisms to determine customer satisfaction.
6. Ensure continuous improvement by establishing a team that measures, analyzes, and completes focused action items.

Once they have completed the necessary groundwork, it's time to get started on the Continuous Improvement program. The secret is to start small and build on your successes. The program can start with one work unit working on one performance indicator, or it can be rolled out to encompass all work units within the company. If the latter approach is chosen, you will still want to start small, with perhaps one team per work unit. The goal is to attain nearly 100 percent participation, but it is unrealistic to do this immediately. It is recommended that you start with, say, less than 20 percent of the workforce. The first teaming activities are going to be learning experiences for everyone involved. As you go up the learning curve, increase the number of teams.

A very positive way to increase participation is to publicize the teams. Give them the opportunity to present the work that they are doing. Giving each team a bulletin board to showcase their results is an excellent motivational tool for both the team members and those not yet on a team. Give them the opportunity to present at monthly communication meetings. "Success breeds success" is an old adage, and it is as true today as it always has been. Let the momentum of the program drive the success of the program.

The basic cycle for continuous improvement teams is shown in Figure S2-1.

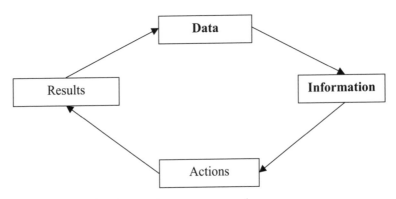

Figure S2-1. Continuous improvement cycle.

Many Six Sigma programs include the DMAIC model, an acronym for Define, Measure, Analyze, Improve, and Control (see Figure S2-2).

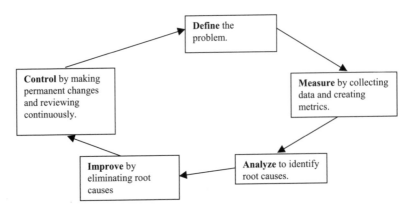

Figure S2-2. The DMAIC model.

The continuous improvement model contained in Section Two provides the transition from either the continuous improvement cycle or the DMAIC model into a practical, hands-on method for implementing improvement programs and attaining desired results.

Most organizations have, literally, tons of data, and yet very few of them are using it effectively. Within this continuous improvement teaming, you will learn how to convert data into information. The tools that will be used to do this are **Pareto diagrams, histograms, scatter diagrams,** and **charting**. Where more information is required, you will learn how to design and implement **check sheets** to gather the data required to provide the sought-for information.

In the beginning of a Continuous Improvement program, you only have visibility on the effect of things that are not being performed well enough to provide high-quality product or service to your customers. You will learn how to use **fishbone diagrams** in conjunction with brainstorming techniques to identify the causes that are responsible for these poor effects. It is by eliminating the causes of poor quality that quality is improved. If the causes are isolated to a specific area, person, or time period within your operation, you will learn **stratification** techniques to identify these unique causes and improve them.

As identified by the Japanese in the late 1960s, the above items shown in bold are known as the seven tools of problem solving. These tools were brought to the United States in 1968, and have been used very effectively in improving the quality of services and goods. These tools do not have to wait for a problem to occur before utilizing them. You will be able to use them to improve your operation and the output of that operation. Thus, we can refer to them as the "Seven Tools of Continuous Improvement."

The Seven Tools

1. *Pareto Diagram*: A graph of rank-order defect data used to prioritize continuous improvement projects and team activities.

2. *Fishbone Diagram*: A framework used to identify potential root causes leading to poor quality.

3. *Check Sheet*: A form designed to collect data.

4. *Histogram*: A graph of variable data providing a pictorial view of the distribution of data around a desired target value.

5. *Stratification*: A method of sorting data to identify whether defects are the result of a special cause, such as an individual employee or specific machine.

6. *Scatter Diagram*: A graph used to display the effect of changes in one input variable on the output of an operation.

7. *Charting*: A graph that tracks the performance of an operation over time, usually used to monitor the effectiveness of improvement programs.

You will learn how and when to use these tools within a logical flow of improvement, from first becoming aware of an operation needing improvement, through identifying root causes, and ending with the action plans required to eliminate the root causes. This will get you the desired results.

Note

1. Kaoru Ishikawa, *QC Circle Koryo* (Tokyo: Union of Japanese Scientists and Engineers, 1980), p. 14.

Step 1: Create the Operational Statement and Metric

Operational Statement

The operational statement is a very concise statement of what you are going to improve. It must be written in simple language with a meaning that is common to everyone who reads it. The simplest definition of an operational statement is, "What's wrong with what." Or, in our usage, "What is not good enough about what." Such is the importance of getting a proper operational statement, that it is not unusual for a team to take as many as three meetings to arrive at an operational statement that meets all of the criteria.

The three criteria for a good operational statement are:

1. It must be *stated in terms of the effect of what it is that you are improving.*
2. It must be *described in terms that have common meaning and understanding.*
3. It must *define the limits of what is to be improved.*

To elaborate on these criteria:

❑ *Stated in terms of the effect of what it is that you are improving.* All interactions associated with the delivery of product or service have an effect on the customers. You are looking at where those effects are less than desirable. These effects are the result of upstream causes. All operations, whether in service or product delivery, either delivered to an internal or external customer, have causes that end in results. These are all cause-and-effect relationships. The causes are those things that are done while the work is being performed. The objective of improvement programs is to identify the causes that are not being done in a manner that produces defect-free results and improve how the work is being done. The approach is to build the quality in.

The first step in identifying causes is to start with the observable effects. At this point in time, it is all that you have knowledge of. Start here with the effect. Later we will go through a logical step-by-step process to identify the troublesome causes and eliminate them. It is extremely important that you identify the effect that you want to eliminate; otherwise, you will be chasing the wrong causes. A problem well defined is a problem well on its way to a solution.

❑ *Described in terms that have common meaning and understanding.* Vague statements, such as "The customers are unhappy," can have many different meanings. What makes some customers unhappy may have no effect on other customers. And, unhappy can mean many different things. The statements must use objective language that speaks to how well you are doing in delivering as promised to an agreed-upon customer expectation.

An effective method for this is the "ask why" technique, in which you keep asking why until you reach a point where the statement has an objective, understandable meaning. Some organizations that start with statements like "The customers are unhappy" may in fact never get past this point. They grasp at a few straws, jump to a few false conclusions, and react to incidents as they occur. Finally they fret over why they are losing so many customers.

An "ask why" conversation may go like this:

"The customers are unhappy."
"Why?"
"Because they don't like our product."
"Why?"
"They say our quality is unacceptable."
"Why?"
"Too many units are getting to them in an unsatisfactory condition."
"Why?"
"The bottle caps are leaking."

Now you have a workable what-is-not-good-enough-about-what statement. Everyone knows what a bottle cap is, and everyone knows what a leak is. We still need some clarifying data that will identify the scope of the problem.

The team has just identified the problem that bottle caps are leaking, and they need additional information. Does the data exist from which they can draw this information? If it does, they can do some basic data analysis to identify when it is, where it is, what it is, and how big it is. Has the problem always existed, or did it appear recently? In what regions does it affect customers? Is it local customers as well as remote customers who receive long over-the-road shipments? Do the caps always leak in the same manner, or are some leaks around the seal and some due to cracks? What is the incident rate? Does it affect 1 percent of the product, or 20 percent, or 70 percent? When it happens, does it affect every bottle within a product lot? Does it affect every lot?

If this database does not exist, the team will have to set up data collection points. They will also want to set up some internal data collection points to determine where in the process this problem first appears. Is it immediately after bottle fill? Does it show up in the warehouse? Does it not happen until the bottles are at the customer?

Depending on what the data reveals, the team will want to modify the operational statements. If the data shows that the leaking caps are isolated to one product line, Clean Hair Shampoo, that the average failure rate is 9 percent of the bottles, that in all cases the leaks are around the cap seal, and that the problem is first detected at the end of the fill-and-cap line, then the modified operational statement will be:

"Nine percent of the Clean Hair Shampoo bottles are leaking around the cap seal at the output of the fill-and-cap line."

This statement provides a very clear understanding of when it is, where it is, what it is, and how big it is.

Another example might be an internal service provider. Within a company everyone wants their computer running with absolutely no problems during the time that they are using it. When a problem occurs, they want the

MIS group to fix it immediately. There are not enough MIS resources available to staff to the level required for "immediately." On the other hand, it is realistic to expect an MIS department to fix problems within, say, fifteen minutes. Thus, a good operational statement for an MIS department could be, "Twenty percent of the trouble calls take more than fifteen minutes to fix."

❑ *Define the limits of what is to be improved.* You cannot improve everything at once, but you can improve something at once. Often teams will want to take on a "world hunger" problem, which will lead to frustration and failure. When it involves internal customers, you will get a lot of pressure from everyone to fix all of their problems right away. External customers generally understand that as you initiate improvement programs, performance will begin to improve, and they will begin to see improved service from you.

Perhaps the MIS department is concentrated at division headquarters and is only staffed during day-shift hours, because that is when computers must be kept running at peak efficiency. If this is the case, their operational statement should be clarified to read:

"During day shift at division headquarters, 20 percent of the trouble calls take more than fifteen minutes to fix."

This statement provides a very clear understanding of when it is, where it is, what it is, and how big it is.

Internal and External Defects

Once you have identified what is not good enough about what, you have now identified your customer(s) and what they consider a defect. The improvement techniques are the same for both internal and external customers. Most units within a company service both types of customers. Usually, Continuous Improvement programs start with external customers. These are the ones that pay the bills.

Often you can put in some form of containment actions. These are stopgap inspections designed to catch the noncompliances internally. These are costly in terms of staffing and added cycle time. They are also not as effective as you would like them to be. There have been several studies done showing that 100 percent inspection is about 80 percent effective. *You cannot inspect quality in; it must be built in.* That is the entire focus of Continuous Improvement programs.

Having said this, until you improve your performance, it is necessary to do something to protect external customers from noncompliances. With these inspection points brought into your operation, you can now collect internal data to provide the information that you will need to establish your metrics and track progress. Thus, either internal defects or external defects can be used to monitor and measure the same problematic performance.

Remember, however, where you put in these containment actions. Once the process has been improved to an acceptable level, remove them. Many companies leave these containments in place, and the reason for them is lost in antiquity. This failure to remove unnecessary inspections accounts for a lot of excessive costs, which have a negative effect on the bottom line.

According to a story that appeared in *Trivia* by L.M. Boyd, the British posted a military detachment on the cliffs of Dover in 1803 to watch for Napoleon. He died in 1821. They stopped funding the guard unit in 1927.

Stories similar to this exist all too often in too many companies.

> Rule: *Remove your containments when they are no longer required.*

Typically, people think of manufacturing departments when they think of defects reaching customers and the need for Continuous Improvement programs. While these activities are important, all departments and work units within a company serve a variety of both internal and external customers. Examples of the type of Continuous Improvement programs that have been utilized by administrative and support organizations are:

Administrative and Support Metrics

❏ *Accounting*
Journal voucher accuracy

❏ *Continuous Improvement Teams*
Cycle time of suggestions response
Number of suggestions accepted
Cost savings from suggestions

❏ *Customer Service*
Cycle time of return analyses
Accuracy of analyses
On-time delivery of reports

❏ *Development Engineering*
New product cycle time

❏ *Inventory Control*
Piece part schedule accuracy
Count station accuracy
Stockroom inventory accuracy
Product on-time delivery

❏ *Marketing*
R.F.Q. cycle time

❏ *MIS*
Total released defects
Customer-found defects
Number of days to repair defects
Age of open failures
Number of failures per month
Operations software
Total released defects
Customer-found defects
Number of open problems
Age of open problems
Engineering cost to fix problems
Software failure rate

❏ *Personnel*
Performance reviews on-time percentage

❏ *Purchasing*
Open invoices in AP
Purchased material quality
Supplier base

Material cost savings
Approved lots
On-time delivery
Buyer cycle time
Procurement cycle time

❑ *Quality Assurance*
Accuracy
Timeliness of projects
Cycle time of projects

❑ *Quality Control*
Accuracy of quality reports
On-time delivery of reports

❑ *Tooling*
Requests done on time

❑ *Training*
Completion of training plans
Percent of certified personnel
Percent of hours trained to plan
Quality training percent completed

Metric

A *metric* is the measurement of performance; an *improvement metric* is the measurement of performance over time. Improvement metrics require that data be maintained on the defect rate reaching customers or data from internal inspection or evaluation points. *Defects* are defined as anything that does not conform to the agreed-upon customer requirements. Customer requirements must be established realistically. Customers may want product delivered within eight hours. If distance and shipping logistics make this impossible, then you must negotiate a realistic performance requirement. In this case you find that the shortest possible transit time is twelve hours. You and the customer must agree that this will be your performance standard and the customer's expectation.

Once the agreed-to requirement standard has been defined with the customer, and the evaluation point where data will be collected has been determined, you are ready to establish the continuous improvement metric. An improvement metric contains three elements:

1. A *baseline* is the average of historical performance over the last several months. The time used to calculate the baseline will be dependent on the volume of activity. The larger the database used, the more accurate the baseline calculation will be.

2. A *goal* must be established. The historical Six Sigma rate of improvement goal is a 10× improvement every two years.

3. *Performance* to goal must be measured on an ongoing basis.

Types of Data

Data falls into two categories. It is either variable data or attribute data.

Variable Data

Variable data is data that is taken from a continuous measurement system. It is also referred to as continuous data. It is data that can take on any value over the range of the measurements. Measurements that are variable, or continuous, are ones that measure length, volume, weight, time, voltage, chemical impurities, etc. Given the sensitivity of the measurement system, the values measured can be any number. Human weight is reported in pounds or kilograms; however, with today's technology, it is possible to measure weight to fractions of ounces or grams.

Generally, variable data is taken on a product value that is centered around an ideal target value. If you are selling 1″ screws, then 1″ is the ideal target. When measuring screw length, the value could be 0.095″, 0.096″, . . . 1.004″, 1.005″, or any value between 0.095″ and 1.005″. To illustrate the point, the measurement range has been limited to these values. Of course, if the process were less in control than this, the measurement range values would be broader. If the customer specification is a minimum of 0.098″ and a maximum of 1.002″, then values outside of these limits are considered nonconforming product or a defect. Product within these limits is considered conforming product, or a good unit.

Variable data will be treated in this go/no go manner. If the value is within specification, it is good. If the value is outside specification, it is bad. There are other techniques that deal with variability reduction. Process characterization studies and experimental designs can be employed to increase the number of values closer to the target value. It is rare that a continuous improvement team will encounter the need for these other methodologies. If it occurs, these other techniques are readily available and can be used on an ad hoc basis.

Attribute Data

Attribute data is data that is taken on an outcome that can only have a small, finite number of conditions. A baseball game is either won or lost. These are the only two choices: a win or a loss. There is no continuum of possible values. It does not matter whether you won by one point or seventeen points. If you produce products in the four primary colors, then the only possible values are red, blue, green, or yellow. If the customer ordered red widgets, and the customer receives yellow widgets, it is defective, or nonconforming, product. If the customer receives red widgets, it is good, or conforming, product. If you are guaranteed to have your meal within ten minutes, and you get it within ten minutes, it is conforming service. If it takes more than ten minutes, it is nonconforming service.

Data Requirements

Data must be factual and based on actual observations or measurements. It must be an indisputable fact that everyone can agree on. The source of the information must be reliable, either from an accredited laboratory or a trained employee. It cannot be somebody's in-laws who talked to an old high school friend who said they heard that your customers were receiving bad product. It must be repeatable, such that if the validity is challenged, it can be repeated or observed again. The saying is, "In God we trust; all others bring data."

You must ensure that the data you are using meets the four requirements of *observable, factual, reliable,* and *reproducible.*

Units

You must choose the units that you are going to use to calculate the defect rate within a standard time period. Defect rates are expressed in fraction defective, percent defective, or parts per million (ppm). In one form or another, all of these are fractional calculations. In order to calculate these, you must use the same unit of measurement in the numerator and denominator of the fractions used in your calculations.

Take the example of an ice cream manufacturer mixing ten 1,000-gallon batches of vanilla ice cream each day. These batches are then divided into ten 100-gallon sub-batches. Each 100-gallon sub-batch is packaged into one-gallon containers, which must be filled to the proper container weight as specified by the customer. When the 1,000-gallon batches are blended, they must have the right proportion of ingredients, and they must contain no contaminants. Problems can occur that would affect an entire batch, e.g., wrong mix or contamination. Problems can occur that would affect an entire sub-batch, such as wrong containers being used. Or, problems can occur that would affect an individual one-gallon container, such as intermittent problems with the fill weight.

What are you going to use to calculate the defect rates? If one batch is contaminated at batch mixing, then you could calculate your defect rate for the day to be:

1 batch/10 batches = 1/10 = 10 percent =
   100,000/million (ppm)

or

1,000 gal/10,000 gal =1/10 = 10 percent =
   100,000/million (ppm)

By keeping the units the same in both the numerator (upper) and denominator (lower) of the calculation, you arrive at the same correct answer, that the process destroyed 10 percent of the product that day. If three of the one-gallon containers had lids missing, then you would calculate the defect rate for the day to be:

3 containers/10,000 containers = 3/10,000 = 0.03 percent = 300/million (ppm)

An administrative example is a department that processes one hundred invoices each day. Each invoice contains twenty line items. They have committed to their customers that the invoices will have no mistakes. At the end of the day, the tally for that day's performance is that four of the invoices have mistakes. The manager reviews the data and finds that ninety-six invoices were processed with no mistakes, one invoice had one line item with an error, two invoices had four line items each with errors, and one invoice had two line items with errors. The department could choose to calculate the defect rate two different ways. In order to monitor the overall performance of the department, the manager is interested in the accuracy of the reports that went to the customers. He or she would calculate the day's defect rate as:

4 reports/100 reports =1/25 = 4 percent = 40,000/million (ppm)

The individual workers filling out the invoices would be more interested in how well they perform all of the detailed work that goes into successfully completing a correct invoice. They would calculate the day's defect rate as:

11 line items/2,000 line items =11/2,000 = 0.55 percent = 5,500/million (ppm)

Both of these methods are legitimate. Each of the different ways speaks to the job function that is being measured. The important thing is that you choose your units and stick with them over time. Remember that we are interested in monitoring and measuring improvements. We are not interested in comparing groups or individuals. It would be silly to say that the workers are better people than the manager is because their defect rate is only 0.55 percent while the manager's is 4 percent.

Creating the Metric

By treating variable data as go/no go data and attributing data as either good or bad, we are now ready to establish a metric that is based on a defect rate. This universal method of establishing a metric based on defects instills a mind-set that an organization, work unit, or individuals within the work unit must constantly strive to improve performance, and it provides the foundation for doing this with objective, customer-focused data.

The metric must flow from the operational statement. If your operational statement is, "Customers are receiving nonconforming product," then a metric must be established that measures the defect rate in terms of number of defective units received by the customers, divided by the total number of units received by the customers. If your operational statement is, "Twenty percent of the trouble calls take more than fifteen minutes to fix," then a metric must be established that measures the defect rate in terms of number of trouble calls that take more than fifteen minutes, divided by the total number of trouble calls processed.

You must also demonstrate how the improvement will contribute to the overall success of the enterprise. It may be tempting to work on how to ensure that your favorite soda is always available in the break room vending machines, but this probably doesn't tie into one of the objectives or key performance indicators of the company. You also must verify with your customers that they agree you are working on the right things. If you improve that which you have identified to improve, will the customers be happier?

Using historical data, determine what the baseline performance has been. Baseline performance is the historical average defect rate. If you don't have historical data, start collecting data for some initial period of time in order to set a baseline performance defect rate. From this starting point calculate a performance goal. The performance goal must be both aggressive and attainable. It also needs to be ever-improving. Do not expect a team to instantly go from a 10 percent defect rate this month to zero next month. "Magic pill" goals result in frustration, a sense of "we're failing," and ultimately in failure of the entire program.

These programs, and goals associated with them, must be continuous and long term. A goal that meets these requirements is the Six Sigma rate of improvement goal. The Six Sigma rate of improvement goal is a ten-fold improvement every two years. Thus, if a team is at a 10 percent defect rate this month, two years from now they should be at a 1 percent defect rate. If a team is at a 4,000 ppm defect rate this month, they should be at a 400 ppm defect rate two years from now.

You must also decide the standard time units that will be used for calculating the defect rate. Typically, teams will calculate their performance on a weekly basis, and management will want to see a monthly calculation. This is case dependent based on the activity level. A good rule of thumb is that there should be at least one hundred units processed before calculating a defect rate. If a work unit is producing twenty-five reports a week, it is best to calculate defect rate monthly. If a work unit is producing a hundred reports a week, the team can choose to calculate performance weekly with a monthly calculation for management. If a work unit is producing 200 reports a day, it is still best to calculate weekly and monthly. Calculating defect rates with too short a time span or not enough activity between calculations will result in wide swings that are both misleading and frustrating.

Metric Example

> *Operational statement:* "Customers are receiving non-conforming product."
>
> *Historical data:* Last year 12,373 units were shipped, and 545 units were defective.
>
> *Baseline performance:* Defect rate = 545/12,373, or 4.4 percent
>
> *10×/2 years improvement goal:* Goal = 4.4 percent/10, or 0.44 percent

A graphic illustration of the improvement goal is shown in Figure 4-1.

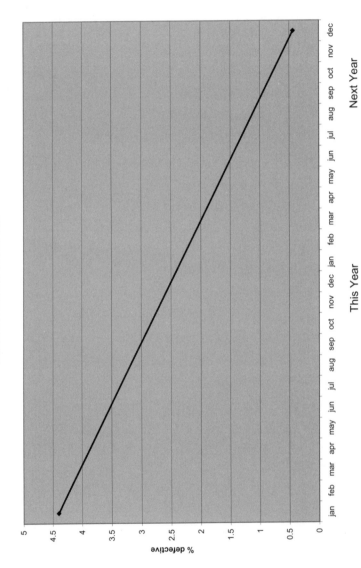

Figure 4-1. Sample improvement metric.

Before you leave Step 1, have you:

❑ Written your operational statement?
❑ Put any required containment actions in place?
❑ Flagged your containments for later removal?
❑ Created your metric and trend chart?
❑ Established a method for collecting your data?

σ

CHAPTER 5

Step 2: Define the Improvement Teams

Identifying the Required Teams

When initiating a Six Sigma Continuous Improvement program, you must prioritize improvement actions and establish teams to work on the predominate reasons for customers receiving defective products or unsatisfactory service. Once a Continuous Improvement program is established and running well—typically six to nine months following initiation—effective teams will be in place. The alignment then shifts from assigning team members to problems to assigning problems to teams. During both of these phases, problems must be addressed on a priority basis. The ideal tool to use for this activity is a Pareto diagram.

Pareto Diagram

A Pareto diagram is a bar chart that displays the reasons for defects, and the number of defects for each reason or category. The Pareto diagram is based on the Pareto principle, which states that 80 percent of all effects can be attributed to 20 percent of the causes. These causes are referred to as the significant few among the insignificant many.

Looking back at the sample metric in Step 1 (Chapter 4), we know that there were 545 defective units received by the customer. The next step is to determine why they were defective. We must determine the reasons for the defects and count the number of defective units within each category. We must choose a consistent time frame in which to count the defects. This will ensure that we have an apples-to-apples comparison. If you count defects for some categories over an entire year and defects for other categories for a month, the results will be skewed and misleading. Choosing a time frame is situational dependent. The time frame must be long enough to capture enough defects to display the natural occurrence of defect reasons. There is no hard-and-fast rule; however, a good rule of thumb is to have at least fifty individual occurrences. The larger the number of data points, the greater the distinction between categories. This will increase your confidence that you have identified the significant reasons and have prioritized your resources properly.

If historical data exists, as it does in most cases, look back to the recent history and choose a time frame that includes enough data points to provide the distinction among defect categories. If historical data does not exist, you will need to establish a check sheet (which will be described in Step 4) to collect enough data to provide the required distinction.

The metric example in Chapter 4 shows that there were 545 defective units last year. It is not necessary to analyze all of this data. For efficiency, you will very likely get enough information from the last quarter of last year. In this example, when the details are looked at for October, November, and December of last year, they reveal the following categories and the number of defective units within each category:

Category	Number of Defective Units
Broken Component	6
Fractured PC Board	34
High Resistance	14
Dented Case	77
Power Cord Missing	5
Illegible Markings	4
Total	140

Now, arrange this list with the most frequent occurrence at the top descending to the least frequent occurrence.

Category	Number of Defective Units
Dented Case	77
Fractured PC Board	34
High Resistance	14
Broken Component	6
Power Cord Missing	5
Illegible Markings	4
Total	140

Start the Pareto diagram by drawing a horizontal axis with the most frequent occurrence at the left and continuing to the right in descending order of occurrence, as shown in Figure 5-1.

Dented Case	Fractured PC Board	High Resistance	Broken Component	Power Cord Missing	Illegible Markings

Figure 5-1. Pareto diagram: horizontal axis.

The next step is to add a vertical axis with a scale high enough to include the largest value. The highest number of occurrences is 77, so the scale maximum will be set at 90 (see Figure 5-2).

You now have a clear picture of the reasons for your customer complaints. Establishing a continuous improvement team to eliminate the dented case and fractured PC board defect rate will eliminate 79 percent of the problems getting to the customer. At this point you must decide how many resources will be assigned to work on continuous improvement projects. Ultimately, the goal is to have 80 percent of the workforce participating on continuous improvement teams, but this takes time. Many companies start small and build to the 80 percent level over a one-year period. If you identify only enough resources to support one team, you would create a team to improve dented cases. If you identify enough resources to support two teams, you would add a team to improve fractured PC boards. If you identify enough resources to support three teams, you would add a team to improve high resistance.

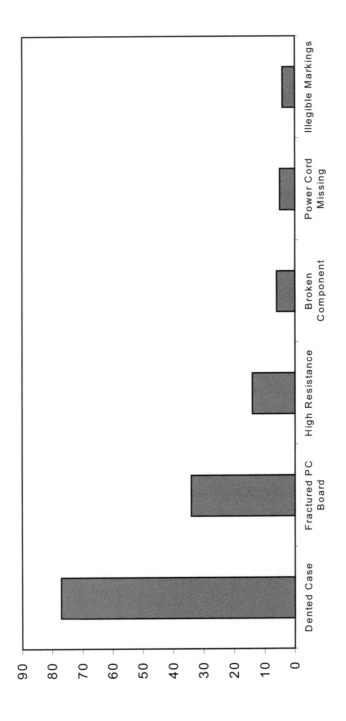

Figure 5-2. Pareto diagram of customer nonconformances.

Sub-Paretos

We have used the high-level data to categorize the reasons for customer complaints, and have used that analysis to identify the required continuous improvement teams. Once the teams are established, they will often need to do the next level of Paretos. These are called sub-Paretos. Usually, two levels are sufficient; however, there will be cases where three or more levels of Paretos need to be completed. This technique complements the "ask why" method of getting to a root reason for defects.

In this example, the dented case continuous improvement team will want to look at the rejects and determine where the dents are occurring. A Pareto analysis of this data will focus the team in the right direction to ferret out and eliminate the root cause(s) behind these defects.

There are any number of possible outcomes from this. If one location, say the top left on the back of the case, is dented at a much higher rate than anywhere else, then the team would look for handling or packaging issues that could lead to that result. If the dents are randomly and consistently spread over the entire surface of the case, then the team will have to investigate for causes affecting the entire manufacturing, packaging, and shipping of the cases.

Staffing the Teams

Before you establish teams, you must get consensus from all levels of management and supervision. Corporate senior management must agree that teaming is something that they will support as part of the enterprise's culture. Middle managers must be aware that their roles will change, and they must be willing to rethink how they lead people. Supervisors must be willing to transition from a control management style to a participative management style.

The early attempts at continuous improvement teams were based on volunteers. This had the drawback of often not having the right skills, experience, and knowledge on the team. Most of these teams accomplished little or failed altogether. In forming teams, you must assemble the right mix of education, experience, and knowledge. People can be motivated to be on a team. The benefits of team participation are improvements in personal skills, recognition for one's efforts, a sense of accomplishment, getting to know more people from different organizations within the company, and small concrete rewards such as movie tickets or a night out on the town.

Motivation is the best way to staff a team. If this fails to get everyone needed, the additional necessary people must be "volunteered" army style. It has been my experience that initially about 20 percent of the workforce will eagerly volunteer. Another 30 percent, perhaps the shy ones, will eagerly say yes when asked. From this beginning, the program will grow. People will see the camaraderie and high spirits of the team participants. This will result in another 30 percent asking to be on teams. This growth to the 80 percent participation level takes from six months to one year. As the teams grow in number and the percentage of employee participation grows, keep the teams intact. After a team completes a successful continuous improvement project, assign them a new project. Ultimately the Six Sigma program will reach the point where teams themselves identify their next continuous improvement project.

The last 20 percent are best to leave alone. If you force

everyone to be on a team, you are going to destroy the very atmosphere that you are trying to create. An 80 percent participation rate is sufficient to declare it a win, establish the culture, and reap the benefits.

Within many work units, workers perform as specified by supervisors; however, it needs to be recognized that the individuals performing the job know how best to do it. These workers are aware of things that are preventing them from doing the job better. There is a lot of native intelligence within all work units that must be utilized to improve performance, maximize efficiency, and produce the highest output quality. These work units have knowledge that does not exist anywhere else in the organization. If only asked, all workers, with very few exceptions, are willing to apply their knowledge and energies to improve performance of the company.

Team members must be trained on the improvement tools and how to apply them for successful results; this must be done when they are eager for the knowledge. Some companies have conducted a massive training program before launching an improvement team program. This often leads to employees not understanding what it is that they should have been learning, and forgetting most of what they did pick up before ever getting a chance to use it. The best programs are those where the improvement team program and required training are launched simultaneously. Prior to this, it is advisable to have a cadre of facilitators trained and ready to assist the teams through their first improvement project.

Team membership should be from three to eight participants, including the leader. Arguably, two people could comprise a team, such as in doubles tennis; however, this is too few to achieve team synergy. Once a team grows to ten members, it is best to break it into two smaller teams. With ten or more people, some team members will drift into anonymity and will not contribute to team activities or success.

Managers can name the team leaders or the team can select the team leader by consensus. Do not let a person who is in a hierarchical position over any of the team members become the team leader. This will only result in delegation and management as usual. The role of the leader is to pull the team members together as a team, call the meetings, ensure attendance, ensure that the inputs and workloads are shared by all team members, and interface with the team champion when necessary. Once a team has successfully completed their improvement activity, the existing team leader should step down and a new one selected for the next project.

Be patient. In the beginning, you are going to need to look at a lot of team glasses as "10 percent full." This is where leadership of the enterprise makes a huge impact. Do not expect "magic pill" solutions.

Team member commitment is for two hours a week—one hour of meeting time and an additional hour to complete team actions. This is done during normal working hours. I have been involved in programs where hourly workers volunteered to come in on their own time without compensation simply because they were excited and committed to what they were accomplishing. Managers may worry, understandably so, about what will happen to the productivity of their group if 5 percent of their time is focused on something other than their traditional work. In all cases that I have experienced, productivity, as measured by output per person-hour, has increased. After studying the case where manufacturing costs decreased by 30 percent, the work unit managers and director of manufacturing came to the conclusion that all workers have a lot of discretionary time during a normal workday and that this time was being better utilized. When people are excited and committed, they spend more time performing tasks central to the success of the enterprise and less time "gathering around the water cooler." Also, as team-driven improvements kick into place, operations become more efficient. There is less scrap, less rework, less wasted motion, which means that efficiency, and resulting cost improvements, is a natural result of improvement team programs.

In the beginning there is resistance to team membership. "I don't have time." "I'm too busy." "We have to get product out the door." These are typical reactions before people become involved. In the beginning they must be reminded that things are not as good as they should be. The challenge is to convince employees that if they keep working forty hours a week doing things in a less than optimal way, they are always going to be working in a less than optimal way. Dedicating two hours a week to improving the status quo is going to improve their working conditions.

John Cotter, a prominent sociotechnical system consultant, found that "in a review of organizations that had transitioned to teams in seven countries,

❑ 93 percent reported improved productivity.
❑ 86 percent reported decreased operating costs.
❑ 86 percent reported improved quality.
❑ 70 percent reported better employee attitudes."[1]

Determining Required Skills and Knowledge

When initiating a Continuous Improvement program, you need to identify the team members required for each improvement project. These do not need to be listed by name; rather, they should be identified by job functions or special skills needed. If a team will potentially be dealing with very technical issues, then an engineer or technologist will be needed on the team. If the scope of operations involved in producing the product or service involves many different work units, then there must be a member from each of these work units.

It is essential that the team is comprised of enough members to handle the work assignments and action plans. If occasionally short-term assistance is needed from people not on the team, it is possible to obtain their assistance without making them team members. The person could be invited to one team meeting in order to provide the required information and answer questions, or a team member could be assigned the action item to interview the person and bring back the required information. Also, look for situations where permanent team members may need to be added from other work units.

Roles and Responsibilities

Each continuous improvement team requires a *team leader, team recorder*, and *team members*. In addition to these core team members, a team also requires a *champion* and a *facilitator*.

Team Leader

The team leader, in conjunction with team members, sets the schedule and venue for team meetings, and ensures that they are held. He or she heads the team meetings, keeping the team focused on the continuous improvement project and monitoring progress against goals. The team leader cooperatively assigns action items and agrees on scheduled completion dates. When the team needs assistance from the champion, the team leader contacts the champion. A good team leader makes sure that all team members are engaged and active in achieving the goals that the team has established. The team leader must also create an environment where all team members are treated with respect and there is no fear within the team.

Team Recorder

The team recorder assists the team leader by keeping meeting attendance records and meeting minutes. Following each meeting, he or she publishes the meeting minutes, which must include the action plan and status of completion to goal. The team recorder also keeps the metric updated so that the team can monitor its progress to goals.

Team Members

Team members must participate in the meetings, accept action item assignments, and complete tasks to schedule. During the meeting it is important that all team members contribute ideas and information that will be beneficial in achieving the desired improvements. Between meetings each team member must spend a minimum of one hour completing action items and working on team objectives. Team members must treat each other with respect. Everyone must feel comfortable voicing his or her inputs.

Champion

The champion is a member of senior management. This person sponsors the team, and is viscerally committed to the team's success. The champion provides financial support for the team's activities. The amount of money is very minimal. Expenses may cover a recognition lunch when the team completes certain milestones, or a small reward such as movie tickets or dinner for two for each team member when they successfully complete their project.

The champion also is called on to break down barriers when necessary. Teams often run into resistance, usually from the middle management ranks. It is sad, but reality, that some people become irrationally territorial and prevent teams from implementing solutions affecting their areas. Others are very image conscious, and are embarrassed when others uncover problems that they feel they should have discovered.

The intent of adding teams is to cooperatively work with everyone in the enterprise to achieve higher levels of performance and success. When irrational roadblocks are encountered, the champion must assist the team by bringing these to a mutually beneficial solution.

Often teams will identify solutions that alter the procedures and practices of an entire operation or a work unit within the operation. In order to implement such solutions, policies must be changed, documents must be rewritten, and/or physical changes need to be made. These broad sweeping changes will require the champion's assistance and support.

Facilitators

Facilitators are key to the success of an effective continuous improvement team program. Facilitators are especially valuable during the early stages of development. The best way to visualize the facilitator's role is to look at the Blanchard Situational Leadership model.[2] Section Three of this book contains a summary of how this model can be applied to the leadership of continuous improvement teams. In the S1-Directing phase, when teams are forming and learning new skills, training is required to give the people the tools that they need, and structure is required to provide an opportunity for them to apply the new skills. In the S2-Coaching phase, teams are developing but lack the competencies required to be self-sufficient. Teams require direction and encouragement. These two phases comprise the primary realm of facilitators.

A good facilitator is familiar with all of the problem-solving tools and the continuous improvement model to tie the tools together in a focused, results-oriented manner. A facilitator must have excellent people skills and teaming skills. A facilitator is part trainer, part leader, part coach, part mentor, and part cheerleader. He or she must know when to be active and when to be passive—when to step in and lead the team and when to sit back and let the team run with the process.

It is important to train and create a cadre of facilitators to aid the teams in working the continuous improvement process, determine their goals, and achieve the desired results. It is best to identify and train these individuals early in the program, preferably before forming teams and chartering them with continuous improvement goals.

The facilitator is not a team member but acts as a guide when the team needs assistance. In the early phases of a team's growth, the facilitator should attend every meeting. As the team becomes experienced and effective in team dynamics and the application of tools, the facilitator should attend an occasional meeting to show continuing support. The team must know that the facilitator is always on call for consultation and assistance. The facilitator must be knowledgeable of problem-solving tools and teaming skills.

Candidates to become facilitators can come from all walks of life. They can reside within any work unit and occupy any level within the company. Attributes to look for in facilitators are excellent interpersonal skills, the ability to listen, and being comfortable in a support role. The candidates then need to be trained in interpersonal skills, effective meeting skills, and continuous improvement quality tools and techniques.

Facilitators work in conjunction with and support of the team leader. They may need to step in to resolve conflicts in a healthy and positive manner. When a team is stuck, the facilitator needs to ask questions, lead brainstorming sessions, recommend a methodology required to get to the next steps for team success, and engage the champion if required.

Rules of Conduct

Teams must predetermine how they are going to resolve conflicts, how decisions will be reached, what behaviors are expected from each team member, and what behaviors are considered inappropriate. There must be an atmosphere of mutual trust and a common vision of what the goal is. A good operational statement will establish the goal. It is imperative that each team member is committed to the goals and feels that by attaining them things will improve. During the meetings it must be understood that each member will give and receive feedback.

Each team member must maintain an open mind. He or she must listen to the ideas of others before commenting on them. Discussion and clarification are healthy within a team; belittling others' ideas is not. The main reason for forming a team is to bring together people with very diverse backgrounds, different education levels, and differing levels of experience. This requires that everyone be respectful of one another and realize that, although each team member's perception may be different, their input is sincere and valid.

Conflicts must be resolved quickly. This may require the services of the team facilitator. Bring the issue out in the open, and let each party state their position and the reasons for their position. Then focus the team on the team goals and why each position has some merit in achieving those goals. Look for the common ground. Remind the participants that they all share a common goal, and ask how they can combine those different approaches into a best solution.

Decisions must be reached with *consensus*. Consensus has many definitions. It is not necessary that everyone embrace the decision with enthusiasm; however, it is important that everyone support it. The best definition of consensus presented to me was by Dr. Jack Null, retired Superintendent of Fowler School District, Phoenix, Arizona, who stated that "everyone must, as a minimum, leave here committed to not undermine the efforts of those supporting this decision."

Teams must work under the guidelines of good teaming practices. The following ingredients for successful teaming were taken from *The Team Handbook: How to Use Teams to Improve Quality.*[3]

1. *Clarity of Team Goals.* A team works best when everyone understands its purpose and goals. If there is confusion or disagreement, they work to resolve the issues. The goals are the larger project goals as well as individual goals, so everyone is focusing on an agreed-upon outcome.

2. *An Improvement Plan.* Improvement plans help the team determine what advice, assistance, training, resources, etc., it may need. They guide the team through determining schedules and milestones, and celebrate successes. These plans are subject to revisions as needed and have some form of documentation describing the process steps.

3. *Clearly Defined Roles.* Teams operate most efficiently when they tap everyone's talent and each party understands their role in producing specific results. This should establish shared responsibility.

4. *Clear Communication.* Clear communication means good, open discussions occur insuring the information [that] is passed between team members. This involves the skills of responsive listening, clarifying and confirming, and using appropriate questions.

5. *Beneficial Team Behaviors.* Team members should initiate discussions, seek information and opinions, suggest procedures for reaching goals, clarify or elaborate on ideas, test for consensus, summarize, encourage participation from everyone, keep discussions from digressing, be willing to compromise, ease tension in the group, and praise others' achievements.

6. *Well-Defined Decision Procedures.* Decision making should be discussed to decide the best ways of making decisions. Options include consensus, decision by a few, voting, polling, and majority rule.

7. *Balanced Participation.* Balanced participation recognizes that every team member has a stake in the group's achievements; therefore, everyone should participate in discussions, decisions, commitment, and project success.

8. *Established Ground Rules.* Ground rules are written to define what will and what will not be tolerated in the group. From time to time review the ground rules, adding, deleting, or revising them as needed. Be sure to pay attention to them when resolving conflicts.

9. *Awareness of the Group Process.* All team members must be aware of the group process—how the team works together. This is being sensitive to nonverbal communication and silence. These may mean that someone is uncomfortable with the discussion, does not trust what is being said, or has a different view. They need to be inquired about so trust and open communication can grow.

10. *Use of the Scientific Approach.* Teams that use the scientific approach rely on good reliable data for decision making. The scientific approach insists that opinions are supported by data.

Before you leave Step 2, have you:

❏ Completed your Pareto diagrams?
❏ Completed any required sub-Paretos?
❏ Identified and assigned all required team members?
❏ Selected a team leader?
❏ Assigned a team champion?
❏ Assigned a team facilitator?
❏ Completed teaming skills training?
❏ Established team rules of conduct?

Notes

1. Kimball Fisher, *Leading Self-Directed Work Teams* (New York: McGraw-Hill, 1993), p. 22.

2. Kenneth Blanchard, Patricia Zigarmi, and Drea Zigarmi, *Leadership and the One Minute Manager* (New York: William Morrow, 1985).

3. Adapted with permission from Peter R. Scholtes, et al., *The Team Handbook: How to Use Teams to Improve Quality* (Madison, Wis.: Joiner, 1988), pp. 6-10–6-22.

σ

CHAPTER 6

Step 3: Identify Potential Causes

Flowcharting

You now have "what is not good enough about what" identified and improvement teams established. Before you start the actions to improve "what is not good enough about what," you need to determine if you need all of the steps, policies, and practices currently in place to produce the service or product for your customer(s). You do not want to waste time improving things that are unnecessary or detrimental to delivery of high quality performance. In addition to improving quality, eliminating unnecessary steps will reduce costs and shorten cycle times.

The best method for doing this is flowcharting. Even for enterprises not engaged in a Continuous Improvement program, it is a good idea to flowchart your operation at least once every two years. Systems and practices left on their own have a way of growing astray.

When you initially designed and implemented your flow for producing the services and products that your customers expect, you started out with a good solid plow horse that could deliver straight rows all day long. You think you still have a plow horse that just isn't performing like it used to. But, when you step back and do an objective, well-informed diagram, or flowchart, of what it is that is actually being done on a daily basis, you discover that your plow horse has metamorphosed into a camel. It's kind of ugly with unnecessary lumps, a bad disposition, and a nasty habit of spitting at you at the most inopportune times. No wonder your rows are crooked. Flowcharting will enable you to see the camel for what it is. You can now restore the camel back to the horse you thought you had.

You will not be wasting time improving a camel that you didn't want in the first place. You will be efficiently using your time and resources in improving the horse that you want and need in order to satisfy your customers.

There are two basic types of flowcharting—*linear flowcharting* and *interdepartmental flowcharting*. Both of these methods will initially yield an "As Is" status. You will then need to identify what it "Should Be." Before proceeding with the next steps of continuous improvement, you must reengineer your system from the "As Is" state to the "Should Be" state; that is, you must change the camel into your horse. And improve the horse.

For our flowcharting we will be using the simplest system of symbols.

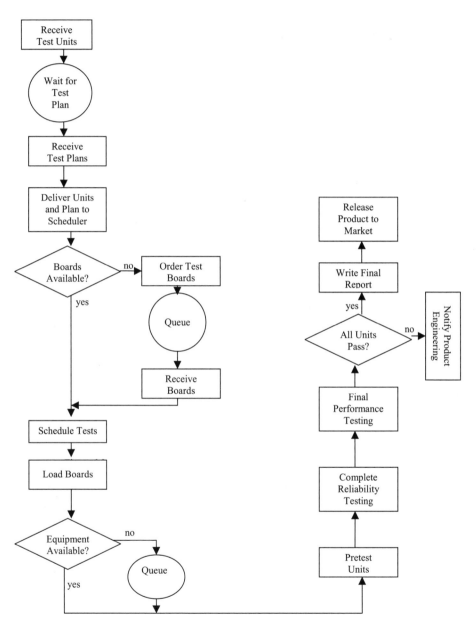

Figure 6-1. "As Is" flowchart for reliability testing.

pretest rejects for over a year. The customer and the lab personnel decided to eliminate pretesting the units.

The scheduler then asked whether there was some way that the lab could get advance notice on when test units would be submitted. Product engineering said that they constantly had several products in design and development, and that they had a good idea of when units of a particular product would be submitted to the lab. In fact, product engineering already had an internal report that predicted when units would be submitted to the lab. It was agreed that weekly they would send a copy of the report to the lab scheduler.

Everyone was in agreement that it had been an excellent meeting. It was felt that this was an excellent example of getting the customer involved in the solutions necessary to provide superior service.

The team then looked into why there was a shortage of test boards. They had to work with the restricted number of test boards that could be kept in inventory. When one of the team members took the action item to ask the department manager about this, the manager chuckled and said the restriction was put in place two years ago during an industry downturn, when cost-cutting measures were imposed. The restrictions no longer made sense. He challenged the team to provide him a proposal for min/max inventory levels that were needed so that they would never again have to wait for a test board. The team submitted the plan, and the department manager, after ensuring that his budget covered the costs, approved the plan.

Subsequent financial analysis showed that this change actually saved the company money. Due to the pressure to get new products out the door as quickly as possible, lab personnel had been placing expedite orders with the board supplier. These orders had a 40 percent expedite charge and were occurring at a high rate. On average, the cost of boards had been higher than normal.

Following these changes to policies, practices, and procedures, the team created the "Should Be" flowchart (see Figure 6-2) and implemented the changes in the reliability laboratory. They still had plenty of things to improve, such as internal scheduling, equipment maintenance, staffing, and training, but now they wouldn't be wasting their time fixing things that weren't needed or no longer made sense.

Interdepartmental Flowcharting

The interdepartmental flowcharting method is used when two or more departments or work units are involved in producing the service or product. In this method, you concern yourself with the hand-offs between departments, the disconnects that can exist, the confusion of who is responsible for each step, and the redundancies that can exist when more than one department is involved.

This example is of a small technical company that was losing business because it took too long for the customers to receive a response when they requested a quote. In many instances, the customers received no response at all. The request for quote, RFQ, should take no more than three working days. The operational statement for this team was, "It takes more than three days to respond to the customer on 80 percent of the RFQs from customers."

The team was composed of members from sales, customer service, purchasing, production control, technical support, and production. All of these departments were

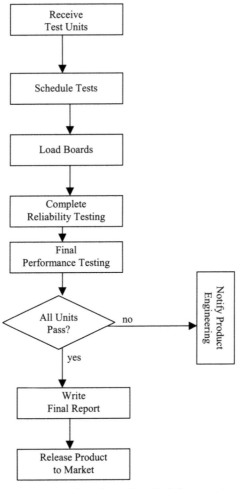

Figure 6-2. "Should Be" flowchart for reliability testing.

involved in processing a quote for delivery to the customers. The team met and created the "As Is" flowchart
for processing a RFQ through the internal system (see
Figure 6-3). Their first observation was that the request
spent a lot of time traveling back and forth between cus-

tomer service and other departments. One of the longest delays in getting quotes out was the amount of time spent by technical support when a nonstandard part was requested. Further discussion revealed that less than 5 percent of the requests were for nonstandard product. The general guideline for process flows and system designs is that if something occurs less than 10 percent of the time, remove it from this flow and create a separate system to handle these exceptions. Sales asked why so many RFQs were entered through departments other than sales. The sales account managers were adamant that all RFQs should come through them.

The customer service manager stated that she was responsible for getting RFQs processed through the plant and getting answers back to customers. RFQs were returned to customer service at every step of the way so that her people could keep track of where they were in the process. After much discussion it was agreed that everyone would trust the other departments to do what was necessary to get the RFQs through the system as quickly as possible. A standard flow for RFQs was developed with a clear understanding of what each department needed to do. Besides, as was pointed out by many team members, this back and forth transfer to customer service was adding a lot of unnecessary time. It was agreed that the RFQs would transfer to the next department where value-add input was required.

Everyone agreed that the account managers should receive and initiate all RFQs from their customers. They were the people closest to the customers and had the knowledge necessary to know which RFQs the company did and did not want to respond to. When asked why the

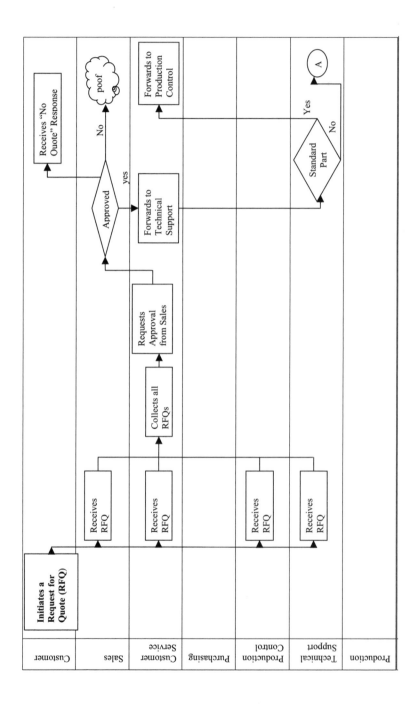

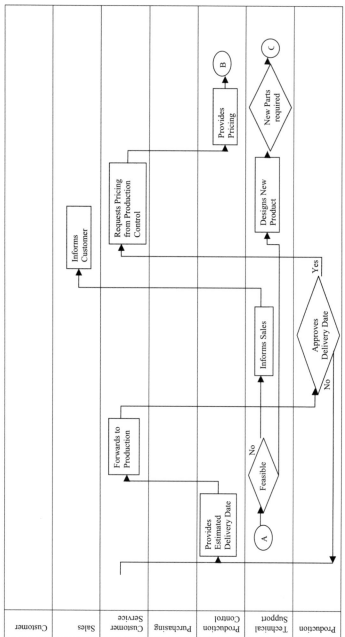

(continues)

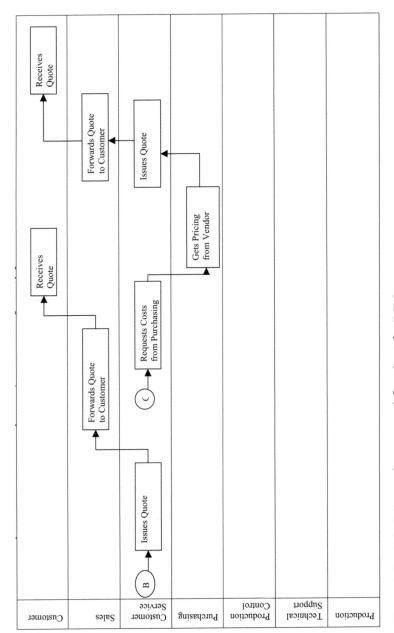

Figure 6-3. "As Is" interdepartmental flowchart for RFQ.

present situation called for sales being bypassed so often, the response was that the previous sales manager, no longer with the company, had set a policy that he didn't want his people involved in what he considered a mundane task. Everyone enthusiastically agreed that sales would be the one-point contact for inputting RFQs.

Nonstandard requests would be directed to the technical support organization, and they were chartered to develop a system for new product development that would be independent of RFQs.

Production control developed standard pricing sheets and gave them to customer service. Customer service could now determine the pricing without the need for production control involvement on every RFQ. Production agreed to provide production control with weekly updates of factory loading and standard throughput times. With this new information, the production control people could provide realistic delivery dates. Production was still a little leery, but they said that they would give the system a chance to work.

With all of these new changes to policies and practices agreed to, the team then generated the RFQ "Should Be" flowchart (see Figure 6-4). There was still a lot of work to be done, but the team would not be spending energy trying to fix an outdated and ineffective system. With just a few of the departments now involved in processing RFQs, the team was able to reduce the number of team members.

Brainstorming

In Step 3 we are transitioning from the known effect, "what is not good enough about what," to begin identifying potential root causes. A *root cause* is something that if we eliminate it or improve it, the situation and results will improve. During the flowcharting, we identified systemic problems and fixed them. We are now identifying what could be wrong with operations or individual tasks.

Brainstorming is a very simple and effective way to utilize the collective intelligence and knowledge of the team to identify all of the things that must be optimal in order for the results to be error free. Before starting the brainstorming session, write the operational statement on a whiteboard or flipchart where all team members can clearly see it. Explain to the group that our objective is to identify all things that can affect the performance of the operational statement.

The rules of brainstorming are:

1. There are no bad ideas or inputs.
2. We will allow for the absurd.
3. Build off of others' ideas.
4. No discussion or critique is allowed during the idea-gathering phase.

The facilitator of the brainstorming:

1. Gets as many ideas as possible
2. Collects ideas as quickly as they come
3. Solicits inputs from each team member
4. Writes down every idea
5. Seeks clarification if necessary
6. Allows as much time as necessary to collect all inputs

(text continues on page 102)

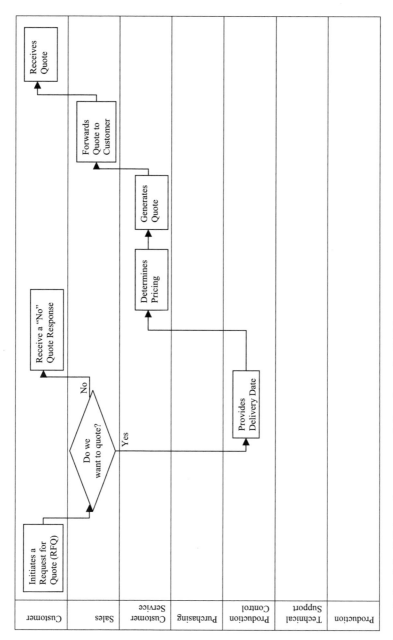

Figure 6-4. "As Is" interdepartmental flowchart for RFQ.

The steps of brainstorming are:

1. Display the operational statement.
2. State the objective.
3. Review the rules of brainstorming.
4. Give the team members a few minutes to think.
5. Solicit ideas from the team.
6. Write down inputs as fast they come in from any team member.
7. If someone has not provided an input, ask him or her for one.
8. After the team as a whole has run out of inputs, go around the table and one-by-one ask each individual whether they have anything more to add. Keep going around the table seeking input from each team member until there are no new inputs.
9. Take a fifteen-minute break.
10. Ensure that there is common understanding on all ideas. If necessary, clarify and restate some ideas.
11. With the agreement of the idea generator and team consensus, eliminate the ideas that were thrown in for fun, are not applicable to the operational statement, or reflect a one-person issue that is not conducive to improving team performance. Any of the latter issues must be handled carefully by a skilled facilitator.
12. With team consensus, group like ideas into one statement.

The list of all items that could affect poor performance as defined by the operational statement has now been generated. At this point in time, all ideas have equal importance. At the end of Step 3, we will prioritize the ideas from the most likely to the least likely root cause.

Fishbone Diagram

An alternative, and often complementary, method for generating the list of potential root causes is the fishbone diagram. In honor of its inventor, it is sometimes called an Ishikawa diagram. The methods for collecting the ideas and the rules for conducting a fishbone diagram session are the same as those for a brainstorming session. The fishbone diagram adds a structure to the generation of ideas. Some people come up with ideas easier in the unstructured brainstorming methodology, while others find it easier to come up with ideas while looking at the structure of a fishbone diagram.

A blank fishbone diagram is shown in Figure 6-5. The operational statement is written within the "head" of the fish. The four major "bones" of the fish are created and

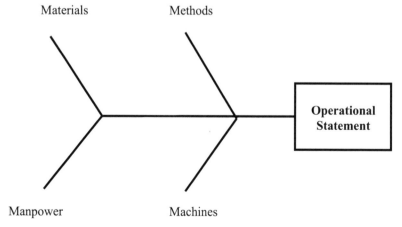

Figure 6-5. Blank fishbone diagram.

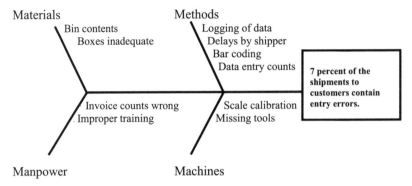

Figure 6-6. Sample fishbone diagram.

labeled for the four generic inputs that are required to successfully complete any operation in manufacturing, administration, or services. These are materials, methods, manpower (we have kept the masculine form to preserve the alliteration), and machines.

As team members come up with ideas, they are grouped onto one of the major bones. These sub-bones can also generate associated ideas that will become sub-bones to the sub-bones. In this manner, the skeleton of the fish is filled in. A simple example of a completed fishbone diagram is shown in Figure 6-6.

Often teams will conduct both a brainstorming session and a fishbone diagram. These are done at two separate meetings at least one week apart. This gives everyone an opportunity to participate using the methodology that they are most effective with. A lot of the ideas will be redundant; however, some additional ones will be generated that did not come up using the other method. At the end of using either method or both methods, the team will have generated a list of all of the things that could be contributing to "what is not good enough about what."

Prioritizing

Generally, the two methods for idea generation will yield somewhere between twenty-five and fifty ideas. Remember that you cannot do everything at once, but you can do something at once. The team must prioritize its activities. By using consensus and voting techniques, the team must pare the list of likely root causes down to the three to five most likely. It has been my experience that teams *always* identify the correct items to improve. I know that they were the correct ones because when they were improved, the desired results were attained.

On flipchart paper taped to the wall, display all of the ideas that were generated during brainstorming and/or fishbone diagramming. Allow ample time and room for consensus-building debates. When everyone is satisfied that they understand each of the idea statements and how they could bring about the desired results, begin the voting process. Each team member should be given ten votes. Team members can vote for as many as ten different ideas, or place all ten of their votes on a single idea, as they wish. Votes can be cast by giving each team member ten sticky dots which they will paste next to the ideas that they are voting for. If you don't have sticky dots, give each team member a marking pen and have them cast their votes by putting a total of ten hash marks next to the ideas that they are voting for. Ties can be broken with a show-of-hands vote.

Sometimes to get the required resolution, it is necessary

to follow the first round of voting with a second round of voting. It will be obvious to the team leader and facilitator when this is required.

Here is an example of the output of a brainstorming session. It was generated by a team that was aiming to reduce the amount of time it took to complete required reliability testing on electronic parts, prior to release for marketing.

Potential root causes generated from brainstorming and fishbone diagramming were:

1. Lack of understanding
2. Work not distributed evenly
3. Computer incompatibility
4. Standard sample sizes
5. Standardize data analysis
6. Midstream changes
7. Grumpy people
8. Only one shift
9. Car problems—late for work
10. Inferior equipment
11. No documented processes
12. Delayed report writing
13. Engineer stressed out
14. Communication gaps
15. Lack of team work
16. Too many projects
17. Project process flow
18. Need new engineer
19. Need automation

20. Need operating instructions
21. Equipment calibration
22. Lack of training
23. Too many hurdles
24. Not in job description
25. Summary data late
26. Mailing list incomplete
27. Checklist for report content
28. No scheduling system
29. Lack of test fixtures
30. Special requests

After prioritizing the list, the top four items that the team began action to improve were:

1. Checklist for report content
2. No documented processes
3. Communication gaps
4. Standardize data analysis

Before you leave Step 3, have you:

❑ Flowcharted the system?
❑ Completed action items identified from flow-charting?
❑ Completed a brainstorming session?
❑ Completed a fishbone diagram?
❑ Prioritized the potential causes?
❑ Selected the three to five most likely potential causes?

Step 4: Investigation and Root Cause Identification

Action Plan

You have identified "what is not good enough about what." You have gathered the necessary data. In most cases there was historical data available, and in some cases teams had to collect new data. Using Pareto charts, you have analyzed the data to identify the major areas of customer dissatisfaction. Using brainstorming and fishbone diagrams, you have identified what the team believes to be the top reasons—the root causes—that are affecting the desired results. By getting to this point, the team has been busy and has completed many tasks. The emphasis now shifts to a focused investigation of the potential root causes. This requires a focused action plan. Action plans have four major components. They are WHAT is to be done, WHO will do it, WHEN is it scheduled to be done, and what is the STATUS of action items, especially the overdue ones.

An action plan document looks like this:

Actions	Responsible	Due Date	Completed	Status
WHAT is to be done	WHO is it assigned to	WHEN is completion schedule	Actual completion date	Comments, historical notes, etc.

For some action items, the responsible person(s) may be the entire team. A team cannot assign action items to nonteam members. When information or action is required from a nonteam member, one of the team members must take responsibility to attain the information or action from that person.

A sample action plan is shown in Figure 7-1. This example is an abbreviated action plan of a team that was chartered with eliminating nonconforming product from reaching the customers. The team's initial review of the data showed that all of the nonconformances that occurred were caused by human error. The output of their brainstorming session and subsequent prioritization of most likely causes was that working conditions and practices in the factory made it very difficult to do error-free work. Notice that they concentrated their actions on training, working conditions, factory cleanliness, and ease of material handling.

Note that the team was concentrating its investigations and fixes on building quality into the product. They did not fall into the trap of assigning blame on an individual;

Action	Responsible	Due Date	Completed	Status
1. Read current procedures applicable to the operation	Team	Mo/Day/Yr		Completed by all except Mary. Her new commit date is Mo/Day/Yr.
2. Provide ideas for more effective job training	Team	Mo/Day/Yr		
3. Review forms in factory for completeness and applicability	George	Mo/Day/Yr	Mo/Day/Yr	16 existing forms reviewed. 3 of them need modification and updating.*
4. Create a training video for factory operators	Mary	Mo/Day/Yr		Mary to meet with manufacturing training department.
5. Install a white-board to communicate procedural changes	Ann	Mo/Day/Yr		
6. Inform each operator of white-board location	Ann	Mo/Day/Yr		
7. Present at weekly production meetings to keep department informed of team activities	John	Ongoing		
8. Modify transportation carts for universal use	Joyce	TBD**		Joyce to obtain commitment from maintenance.
9. Design check sheets for final inspection	George	Mo/Day/Yr		Data will be collected and reviewed weekly.
10. Train final inspectors on use of check sheets and obtain their commitment to use them	George	Mo/Day/Yr		
11. Review product handling practices at manual operations	Mary	Mo/Day/Yr		
12. Initiate factory cleanliness program	John	Mo/Day/Yr		

* Now that this action has been completed, it identified the need for new actions. There are three forms that need to be redone and installed on the factory floor, which will create three new action items to be added to the list as actions 13, 14, and 15.

** TBD stands for To Be Determined. Joyce can't provide a commit date until she has talked to the maintenance supervisor to see when he can schedule the required modifications.

Figure 7-1. Sample action plan.

rather, they correctly concentrated on fixing the system. There was a final inspection in place where detected rejects were removed and reworked for compliance before they were shipped to the customer. It is well known that you cannot inspect quality in, and even if you could, you wouldn't want to. It is a very expensive, nonvalue-add step in any manufacturing flow. Also, the team was not placing blame on any other employee in the company. They were concentrating on root cause reasons of why nonconforming product was being generated, and they were concentrating on positive solutions.

Fix Problems—Not Blame

Action plans are "living documents." As the name suggests, a living document has a life of its own. These Continuous Improvement programs often take months before all the root causes are discovered, solutions are put in place, and the desired results are obtained. As some actions are completed, they will generate new actions. In the sample action plan (Figure 7-1), completion of Action 3 resulted in the generation of three new action items. Also, as the team gets deeper into the investigation phase, they will discover new things that need to be done and new information that must be collected. All of this needs to be captured into a single action plan. As actions are completed, drop them from the action plan by archiving the old version. As needs for new actions are discovered, add them to the action plan. The action plan archives become the history of the team's activities.

Check Sheet

As you continue with your investigation into root causes that are preventing the desired performance, you will need to collect and analyze data. The tool for collecting data is the check sheet. The tools for *analyzing* the data are stratification, histograms, and scatter diagrams. A check sheet is a form used to *collect* data. You must understand your purpose for collecting the data. What questions are you trying to answer, or what are you attempting to get a more detailed picture of? Before you design the form, you must determine what kind of data you are attempting to collect, where the data is to be collected, and the time period over which you want to collect the data. You should have a good idea of what your actions will be depending on what the data shows you. This will help guide you in how to design the check sheet form and where to collect the data. You must also predetermine how you will communicate the data.

The steps in creating and utilizing a check sheet are:

1. Create the form to collect the data, i.e., the check sheet.
2. Determine whether you want to collect data by shifts, by production line, or by individuals.
3. Determine the collection points.
4. Place the check sheet in the active work area(s).
5. Train the workers in how to use the check sheets, and obtain their commitment to fill in the requested data diligently.

6. Collect the information. Check sheets should be collected daily or weekly, depending on the activity level and the amount of data that can be entered into one check sheet form.

7. Continuously review whether the check sheet is working as you intended. If not, modify it as necessary.

8. Digest and analyze the data.

9. Determine the best way to display the data. Is it better to convert it to a Pareto diagram, or a histogram? Will the data be used to identify stratification within the operation?

10. Communicate the findings in your data, especially to those who are collecting it for you.

11. Determine for how long you must collect the data.

Check Sheet Example 1

Your company makes bicycles that are sold through chain stores. There have been many customer complaints about defects, which have resulted in returned product. To get real-time visibility of what types of defects are being produced in the factory, you initiate a final inspection and place a check sheet there. Sales and customer service tell you that there have been many reasons for the complaints. They include bent tire rims, scratched paint, paint runs, dents in the frame, bent frames, inoperative brakes, and inoperative gears.

The check sheet looks like this and is placed at final inspection.

Final Product Defects			
Location: Final Inspection	Collection Time Period	Start Date	End Date
Defect	Occurrence		
Bent Tire Rim			
Scratched Paint			
Paint Runs			
Dents in Frame			
Bent Frame			
Inoperative Brakes			
Inoperative Gears			

Final inspectors have been asked to place an X in the occurrence column for each defect found.

The check sheets are collected each day, and a team member has been keeping a running tally of the defects observed at final inspection. After three weeks of data collection and accumulation, the tallied check sheet looks like this.

Final Product Defects			
Location: Final Inspection	Collection Time Period	Start Date mm/dd/yy	End Date mm/dd/yy
Defect	Occurrence		
Bent Tire Rim	XXXX		
Scratched Paint	XXXXX XXXXX XXXXX		
Paint Runs	XXXX		
Dents in Frame	XXXXX XXX		
Bent Frame	XXXXX XX		
Inoperative Brakes	XX		
Inoperative Gears	X		

It is clear that these defects are occurring in the factory. It is also clear that most of the defects are occurring in the framing shop where the frames are built and painted. Paint runs, bent frames, and dents in the frame can only occur in the framing shop. Scratched paint could occur in the framing shop or in subsequent assembly operations. It is decided that a check sheet must be created and placed at the point where frames are transferred from the framing shop to assembly. Also, the manager of the framing shop wants to be able to see which shifts are producing the defective frames.

The team creates a check sheet for the framing shop that looks like this.

Framing Shop Outgoing Defects			
Location: Framing Shop	Collection Time Period	Start Date	End Date
Defect	Occurrence		
Scratched Paint			
Paint Runs			
Dents in Frame			
Bent Frame			

Note: Use X for day shift, 0 for second shift, and T for third shift.

After three weeks of data collection, the check sheet looks like this.

Framing Shop Outgoing Defects			
Location: *Framing Shop*	*Collection Time Period*	*Start Date*	*End Date*
Defect	*Occurrence*		
Scratched Paint	X T		
Paint Runs	T T T T X T T T T T T T T T		
Dents in Frame	T T O T X T T T		
Bent Frame	T T O X X O T		

Note: Use X for day shift, 0 for second shift, and T for third shift.

The incidence of scratches is much less than was found at final inspection, which indicates that most of the scratching is occurring during assembly. The team will initiate an investigation with the assembly workers to investigate this. The paint runs and dents are prevalent on third shift. This is the shift where most new hires start out, which suggests a need for training. The team members will talk with the third-shift personnel to determine why so many mistakes are being made and what training or assistance they need to rectify the problems. The bent frame occurrences are spread evenly over the three shifts. This indicates some problems with the jigs and presses used to form the frames. The team will contact the maintenance department to assist with investigating this.

Check Sheet Example 2

Your company makes sub-assemblies for the electronics industry. The product is not standard; each customer has unique requirements for each order placed. The parts are built to order, and cycle time is critical. Orders are received, processed, and entered at headquarters in the United States. The manufacturing process starts in the United States, where sub-components are prepared, and then shipped to Honduras for final assembly. From there the sub-assemblies are distributed to a worldwide customer base.

Your commitment, and the customers' expectation, is that orders will be filled within four working days. Performance has not been good; over 10 percent of the orders are shipped late. This is primarily caused by delays clearing product through Honduran customs.

The shipping personnel in the United States are responsible for packaging and shipping the sub-components with the proper paperwork. They are required to send a "prealert" to the receiving personnel in Honduras so that they are aware of incoming shipments and can make sure that they are at customs to receive them as they clear. The company always uses the same air carrier, and the ship-to address is always the same.

Working together, the U.S. and Honduras shipping and receiving personnel form a team to eliminate these delays at Honduran customs. In order to clear customs, each shipment must have the correct count of parts, the value price of the shipment must be correct, the part number and PO number must match between the paperwork and the parts, and the shipment must contain two sets of documents, one in Spanish and one in English. Also, to ensure fast delivery, the Honduran personnel must receive a "prealert."

To determine why the product is being delayed at customs, the team pulls the records from the previous month and creates a check sheet that looks like this.

Product Delays at Customs		
Location: Honduras	*Collection Time Period*	*July Records*
Reason	*Occurrence*	
Wrong PO Number		
No Prealert		
Wrong Part Number		
Wrong Count		
No Spanish Description		
Wrong Pricing		

A review of the records yielded this completed check sheet:

Product Delays at Customs		
Location: Honduras	*Collection Time Period*	*July Records*
Reason	*Occurrence*	
Wrong PO Number	XX	
No Prealert	XXXXX XXXXX XXXXX X	
Wrong Part Number		
Wrong Count	XXXXX XXXXX XXXXX XXXXX XXXXX XXXX	
No Spanish Description	X	
Wrong Pricing	X	

Subsequent investigation found that the operating procedures controlling the shipments to Honduras did not include the requirement for issuing "prealerts." Some of the more experienced personnel knew that they were needed, but not all employees did. The requirement for "prealerts" was added to the operating procedures and all employees were trained.

Another problem that surfaced was caused by the need for speedy processing. Everyone in the warehouse knew that cycle time was paramount. In an attempt to keep things moving fast, they would send shipments even though they did not have enough parts. All personnel were now informed of the export regulation requirements, and this practice was discontinued.

Check Sheet Example 3

Your department receives large runs of piping that must be cut to length and delivered to final assembly, where they are installed into the final product. The specification is that each pipe must be 10 inches long plus or minus ¼ inch. Thus, the lower specification limit (LSL) is 9¾ inches, and the upper specification limit (USL) is 10¼ inches. There have been many complaints from assembly that the pipes are not the correct length. Your customer, in this case an internal customer, is angry.

You have gauging that is capable of measuring the pipes to the nearest sixteenth of an inch. Because employees believed that the cutting jig was accurate enough to make outgoing measurements unnecessary, they never used the gauge. It is now apparent that each piece must be measured before it leaves the shop, and you need to get data that will indicate what the underlying problem may be.

You create a check sheet that looks like this.

Gas Pipe Section Length			
Location: Cutting Shop	Collection Time Period	Start Date:	End Date:
Measurement	Occurrence		
$<9\frac{1}{2}$			
$9\frac{1}{2}$			
$9\frac{9}{16}$			
$9\frac{5}{8}$			
$9\frac{11}{16}$			
$9\frac{3}{4}$			
$9\frac{13}{16}$			
$9\frac{7}{8}$			
$9\frac{15}{16}$			
10			
$10\frac{1}{16}$			
$10\frac{1}{8}$			
$10\frac{3}{16}$			
$10\frac{1}{4}$			
$10\frac{5}{16}$			
$10\frac{3}{8}$			
$10\frac{7}{16}$			
$10\frac{1}{2}$			
$>10\frac{1}{2}$			

After a week of measuring all of the pipes leaving the cutting shop, the check sheet filled in like this.

Gas Pipe Section Length			
Location: Cutting Shop	Collection Time Period	Start Date: dd/mm/yy	End Date: dd/mm/yy
Measurement	Occurrence		
$<9\frac{1}{2}$	XXX		
$9\frac{1}{2}$	XXXXXXXXX		

$9\frac{9}{16}$	XXXXXXXXXX
$9\frac{5}{8}$	X
$9\frac{11}{16}$	X
$9\frac{3}{4}$	XX
$9\frac{13}{16}$	XXXXXXXXXXXXX
$9\frac{7}{8}$	XXXXXXXXXXXXXXXXX
$9\frac{15}{16}$	XXXXXXXXXXXXXXXXXXXXXXXXXXXX
10	XXXXXXXXXXXXXXXXXXXXXXXXXXXXXXXXXXXXXXXX
$10\frac{1}{16}$	XXXXXXXXXXXXXXXXXX
$10\frac{1}{8}$	XXXXXXXXXXXX
$10\frac{3}{16}$	XXXXXXX
$10\frac{1}{4}$	X
$10\frac{5}{16}$	
$10\frac{3}{8}$	
$10\frac{7}{16}$	
$10\frac{1}{2}$	
$>10\frac{1}{2}$	

The data shows that, in general, the process is capable of producing pipe lengths to specification, and for some reason about 17 percent of the pipes are too short for use. The pipe lengths were produced on two cutting machines operated for one eight-hour shift each day. Subsequent investigation (see "stratification" examples below) showed that the short pipes were being produced from one machine (Machine 1) and were most prevalent toward the end of the day. Further investigation revealed that this machine produced the most parts.

The operator of Machine 1 took great pride in his ability to produce more parts than his coworker. He had received recognition and praise from management for his high productivity rate. Unfortunately, it was discovered that as the day wore on and he was not achieving the output that he expected of himself, he would omit the critical step of cleaning the end plates that clamped the pipe in place. Cutting oil and shavings debris would collect on these plates, and if not cleaned between every cut, the piping would be mounted short. After being counseled on the results of his actions and trained, the operator immediately began religiously following all necessary steps, and the problem went away.

Stratification

Stratification means to look for differences in the sources of variation observed on the output of an operation. Usually, the first step in establishing a check sheet or in analyzing the output data is to think of the output as coming from one homogeneous process. However, this is seldom the case. Most likely there is more than one worker producing the product or service. There may be inputs from different suppliers, different inputs to the process, or multiple machines. The quality of the product or service may depend on the shift on which it was produced or on the time of day within the shift that it was produced.

You will need to consider these variations in the process and analyze your data accordingly. Sorting data by variations in worker, supplier, input, machine, shift, time of day, and/or date will provide stratified information. In the Check Sheet Example 3, after reviewing the initial data, the team decided to look for stratification. Using the same check sheet, they used different symbols to indicate the two machines that were producing the lengths of gas pipe. This showed that stratification was occurring.

Stratification Example 1

Gas Pipe Section Length			
Location: Cutting Shop	Collection Time Period	Start Date: dd/mm/yy	End Date: dd/mm/yy
Measurement	Occurrence		
<9½	OOO		
9½	OOOOOOOOO		
9⁹⁄₁₆	OOOOOOOOOO		
9⅝	O		
9¹¹⁄₁₆	O		
9¾	XO		
9¹³⁄₁₆	XXXXXXOOOOOOOO		
9⅞	XXXXXXXXXXOOOOOOOO		
9¹⁵⁄₁₆	XXXXXXXXXXXXXXXXOOOOOOOOOOOOOOOO		
10	XXXXXXXXXXXXXXXXXXXXXXXXXXXXXXOOOOOOOOOOOO		
10¹⁄₁₆	XXXXXXXXXXXXOOOOOO		
10⅛	XXXXXXXXXOOO		
10³⁄₁₆	XXXXXOO		
10¼	X		
10⁵⁄₁₆			
10⅜			
10⁷⁄₁₆			
10½			
>10½			

Note: O = Machine 1   X = Machine 2

Clearly all of the nonconforming parts are coming from Machine 1. This information is a big step toward identifying the root cause of the problem.

To determine whether there was any variation caused by the time of day that the pipes were cut to length, the team then decided to take a closer look at the output from

Machine 1. The normal shift hours were from 7 AM until 4 PM, with an hour off for lunch from noon to 1 PM. They decided to fill in the check sheet using numbers to indicate the hour during which the pipes were cut.

Gas Pipe Section Length			
Location: Cutting Shop	Collection Time Period	Start Date: dd/mm/yy	End Date: dd/mm/yy
Measurement	Occurrence		
<9½	11, 2, 3		
9½	1, 11, 1, 2, 2, 3, 3, 2, 11		
9⁹⁄₁₆	2, 2, 2, 3, 3, 2, 3, 11, 2, 3		
9⅝	3		
9¹¹⁄₁₆	3		
9¾	3		
9¹³⁄₁₆	3, 2, 10, 7		
9⅞	7, 7, 8, 8, 8, 9, 10, 11		
9¹⁵⁄₁₆	7, 8, 8, 8, 8, 9, 9, 9, 9, 10, 10, 10, 10, 11, 11, 11		
10	7, 8, 8, 9, 9, 9, 9, 10, 10, 10, 9		
10¹⁄₁₆	7, 7, 8, 9, 10, 11		
10⅛	7, 7, 11		
10³⁄₁₆	7, 9		
10¼			

This further stratification of the data indicates that the short lengths are being produced from Machine 1 predominantly in the late afternoon. Armed with this, the team was able to quickly identify the root cause and implement a permanent corrective action.

Stratification Example 2

In another example, the supervisor of production control inventory utilized stratification. The system that was in place was for the receiving dock to accept large shipments of piece parts each day that had to be dispersed to three production lines. Upon receipt, the receiving dock would e-mail production control asking for instructions on the number of piece parts to be delivered to each production-line inventory point. The commitment was that this information would be provided within ten minutes. To keep inventory costs minimal while maintaining production flow, the quickness of this response was critical.

The receiving dock manager received complaints that many of these responses were not happening within ten minutes. After she contacted the supervisor of inventory control about this, he decided to establish check sheets on the response times for each of the three people assigned the responsibility for these responses. This initial data collection by individual would provide stratification. A review of the data provided the following information.

Inventory Dispersal Instructions Response Time			
Location: Inventory Control	Collection Time Period: Last Two Months of Data		
Response Time	Bob	Mary	Gene
<5 min			X
5 min	X	X	
6 min	XXX	XX	XXXXX
7 min	XXXXXXX	XXX	XXXXX
8 min	XX	XX	XXX
9 min	XX	X	X
10 min			
11 min		X	
12 min			
13 min		XX	
14 min		XX	
>15 min		X	

The data shows that all responses over ten minutes were processed by Mary. Can you conclude from this that Mary is a poorer performer than Bob or Gene? No! Mary was the most experienced and knowledgeable employee, and investigation revealed that the requests that were incomplete or had erroneous information were passed to Mary for processing. It turned out that the root cause of these problems actually resided with the receiving dock personnel. When they e-mailed the requests, they often inputted wrong part numbers or wrong quantities. The manager of the receiving dock thanked inventory control for this information and initiated a corrective action team of her own.

Histogram

Histograms are another tool for graphically displaying data. They are used exclusively for variable data. The data that is displayed on a histogram can come from a check sheet or from historical data. Cases where you will apply histograms include manufacturing operations where a dimension or measurement is distributed around a central target value with upper and lower specification limits. They also include cases from manufacturing or administrative operations where you are attempting to stay either above or below a minimum or maximum value.

A histogram is used to compare the distribution of data to what is expected, compare the distribution to the specification, and determine what the data image is telling you.

In Sample 1 (Figure 7-2), the process is centered on target and is within specification limits. This is the ideal data footprint.

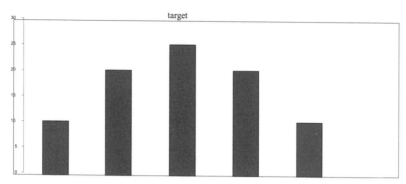

Figure 7-2. Sample histogram 1.

In Sample 2 (Figure 7-3), the process output is being defined by two sets of circumstances. A stratification study must be completed.

In Sample 3 (Figure 7-4), the process is, for the most part, in control and within specifications; however, several of the outputs are abnormally high. An investigation must be completed to determine and eliminate the root cause of these special results.

When creating a histogram, it is important to sort the data into the right number of groups. If you spread

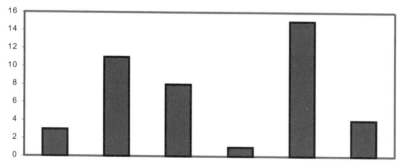

Figure 7-3. Sample histogram 2.

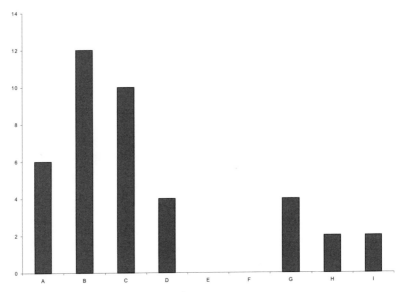

Figure 7-4. Sample histogram 3.

the histogram out with too many groups, you will end up with a flat distribution that will provide no picture of what the data distribution looks like. Similarly, if you have too few groups, the data will all be bunched together. Again, you will have no picture of the data distribution.

The rule of thumb on how many groups to separate the data into is:

Number of Data Points	*Number of Groups*
<50	5 to 7
50 to 100	6 to 10
100 to 250	7 to 12
>250	10 to 20

Histogram Example

Take an example of a process that is designed to fill containers to a weight of 150 pounds. The team wants to determine whether the process is targeted correctly and whether the process is under control. The team weighs the contents of forty-two containers and obtains the following data:

Container Content Weight in Pounds

102	138	132	114	125	123
164	103	162	131	186	192
192	116	187	134	142	137
147	153	144	163	147	151
158	158	182	176	146	143
154	136	154	127	172	145
146	168	156	155	177	196

The first step in creating a histogram is to determine into how many divisions we want to group the data and the range of each division. Using the rule of thumb for histograms, these forty-two data points will be split into five divisions.

The next step is to determine the overall range of the histogram. The lowest reading is 102 and the highest reading is 196, so the overall range of the histogram will be from 100 to 200. The range is 100 pounds wide, and we want to divide it into five divisions. By dividing 100 by 5, we determine that each division will be 20 pounds wide. Thus, the divisions will be:

100 to 120 pounds

120 to 140 pounds

140 to 160 pounds

160 to 180 pounds

180 to 200 pounds

Next we need to count how many data points are in each division.

Division	Data Points	Total
100–120	102, 103, 114, 116	4
120–140	138, 136, 132, 131, 134, 127, 125, 123, 137	9
140–160	147, 158, 154, 146, 153, 158, 144, 154, 156, 155, 142, 147, 146, 151, 143, 145	16
160–180	164, 168, 162, 163, 176, 172, 177,	7
180–120	192, 187, 186, 192, 196, 186	6

The histogram is built by creating bars the width of each division and the height of the total count within each division.

The sample histogram in Figure 7-5 provides a good picture of how the process is running. It is centered on the target of 150 pounds, and looks to be a normal distribution around that target. However, a plus and minus fifty-pound variation seems too high. The team will need to determine how to make the process more repeatable so that container weights are more consistent.

Scatter Diagram

When applying the six steps of continuous improvement, you are investigating what is not good enough about a system for accomplishing tasks or producing product or service. Flowcharting, brainstorming, and fishbone diagrams

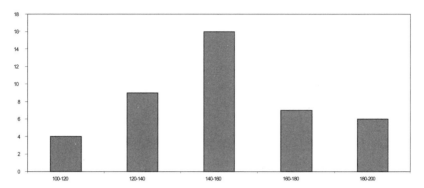

Figure 7-5. Sample histogram 4.

study the causes of poor performance at the *system* level. Stratification and histograms study the causes of poor performance at the *individual* operation or process step. Scatter diagrams study the specific effect that one input variable will have on the output of an operation or process step.

When creating a scatter diagram, you control one of the input variables to a process or operation and measure the performance of one of the output variables. The input variable is referred to as the independent variable. It is the *x* value and will be dispersed along the horizontal axis of the graph. The output that is being measured is the dependent variable. It is the *y* value and will be dispersed along the vertical axis of the graph (see Figure 7-6).

Scatter Diagram Example

Your department is manufacturing specialty chemicals. The customers have been complaining that there is too much variation in concentration. The specification, and customers' requirement, is that concentration variation shall be less than 5 percent. Your team has been working to improve the performance. One of the things that you

Controlled Variable	Measured Variable
Independent Variable	Dependent Variable
The "X" value	The "Y" value
Horizontal Axis	Vertical Axis

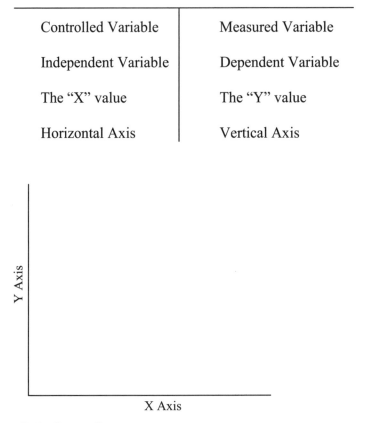

Figure 7-6. Scatter diagram.

suspect is that the higher the temperature of reaction the wider the variation. At present the reaction temperature is set at 110°C. You want to know how variation is affected by either raising or lowering the reaction temperature. The reaction temperature will be set at 100°C, 105°C, 110°C, 115°C, and 120°C. At each of these temperatures, ten batches will be processed and variation from batch to batch will be determined.

The form that you create to collect the data looks like this.

Concentration Variation Study									
Temperature	Percent Variation from Batch to Batch								
	1–2	2–3	3–4	4–5	5–6	6–7	7–8	8–9	9–10
100°C									
105°C									
110°C									
115°C									
120°C									

After running the ten batches at each temperature and determining the variation from batch to batch, the filled-out form looks like this.

Concentration Variation Study									
Temperature	Percent Variation from Batch to Batch								
	1–2	2–3	3–4	4–5	5–6	6–7	7–8	8–9	9–10
100°C	2	3	1	1	2	1	3	2	1
105°C	3	5	4	5	3	3	3	5	4
110°C	4	4	4	5	6	6	7	6	5
115°C	5	5	6	4	7	6	7	5	4
120°C	7	8	6	8	7	8	8	6	7

The scatter diagram created from this data (Figure 7-7) confirms the team's suspicion that the higher the temperature, the greater the variation. Also, by looking at the scatter diagram, it is easy to see that the temperature must be kept below 105°C to keep the variation below 5 per-

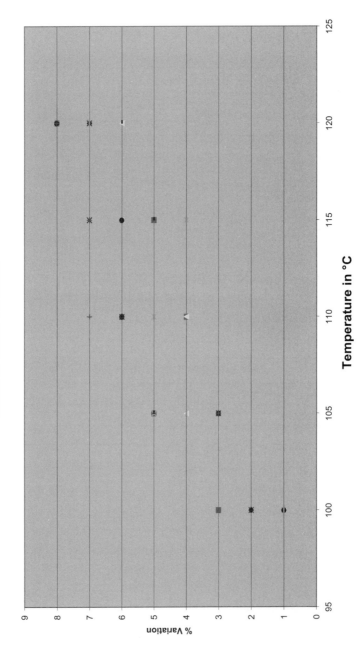

Figure 7-7. Batch-to-batch variation.

cent. At 105°C there is a risk that the variation could go above the 5 percent limit. At 100°C the variation is comfortably within the 5 percent limit.

The team will need to meet with management and the team champion to discuss the next steps. Lowering the temperature from 110°C to 100°C will solve the variation problem, but it will slow down the production rate. Working with production and engineering, the team will need to decide the best course of action to provide the best product to the customer while maintaining the required output rate.

In this example, there are forty-five paired points: nine each at five temperatures. The rule of thumb for scatter diagrams is, to get a true picture of the effect, you must have a minimum of thirty paired points.

The outcome of a scatter diagram can be a positive correlation, a negative correlation, or no correlation (see Figure 7-8). With a positive correlation, as the independent variable is increased, the dependent variable will increase. With a negative correlation, as the independent variable is increased, the dependent variable will decrease. With no correlation, as the independent variable is increased, the dependent variable will neither increase or decrease but will remain randomly dispersed.

Before you leave Step 4, have you:

❑ Created an *action plan* and completed all actions?

❑ Created any required *check sheets?*

❑ Completed *stratification* studies?

❑ Analyzed data using *histograms?*

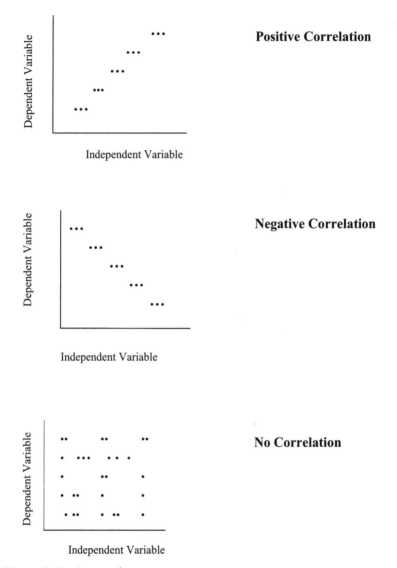

Figure 7-8. Scatter diagram outcomes.

❑ Analyzed data using *histograms?*
❑ Analyzed data using *scatter diagrams?*
❑ Identified the *root causes?*
❑ Verified that elimination of the root causes resulted in improvement?
❑ Achieved your improvement goals?

Step 5: Make Improvement Permanent

Institutionalization

It is imperative that the overall goals and objectives of the business, centered on complete customer satisfaction, fuel all teaming activities. Also, all Continuous Improvement programs are driven by data. This starts with the initial data that determines what is not good enough about what. Undesirable effects are prioritized using a Pareto diagram. Initial teams are formed using this analysis. The teams then use a variety of data collection and analysis techniques to determine the root causes of less-than-desirable results.

Teaming changes the culture of the enterprise. By pulling all employees at all levels together, with one common vision of what is important and what is required to continually strive for better and better performance, morale will improve. Work life will change for all people that use these techniques. Work will become a more productive and satisfying experience. According to Kimball Fisher, "I have seen people at every level of the organization—*even though it sometimes meant personal inconvenience*—decide to do things differently when confronted with the facts."[1]

Team members, predominantly drawn from the hands-on employees, will learn new skills. They will experience a renewed sense of their contributions to the company's performance. As they achieve breakthrough performance and realize that they have learned new skills and have done things that were previously unheard of, they will gain confidence and walk a little taller. Communication with management will improve. They will gain a deep, satisfying appreciation of what is expected of them and knowledge of how their efforts contribute to the company's success.

Middle managers are often perceived, by themselves, to be the most threatened in their positions. Thus, they are often the most resistant to embrace a teaming culture. Those that stick with the process, learn their new roles, and attain the skills necessary for management in an open and sharing manner are the ones that reap the largest benefits. I was in middle management when teaming was first introduced at Motorola. Typical of people in similar situations, I was confused on what this new role would be and what the new rules would be. Over a course of two years, I had to reinvent myself from a command-and-control manager to a teaming manager. The journey had its rough spots; however, the rewards were immense. Sharing information and providing employees with the knowledge that

they needed to improve working conditions and depart-
mental performance created an atmosphere of high morale
and an understanding that we are all in this together.

> A new breed of managers is emerging in America. This new
> breed has discovered and applied a form of management (that)
> is responsive to the changing nature of the workforce and the
> pressures of competition. This is a social invention of such sig-
> nificance that it cannot be ignored by any organization inter-
> ested in its own long-term survival and growth.[2]

Senior management, owners, and stockholders are huge
beneficiaries. As performance increases, costs go down, customers become happy, sales increase, profits increase, and
the company's image in the marketplace and community
becomes very positive. The worth of the company and the
wealth of the stockholders increase.

GE utilizes Six Sigma, and Jack Welsh is a fan.

> What I believe in more than anything is that the whole idea of
> leading is to get every mind in the game. If employees feel their
> ideas count and feel that their jobs are exciting and see the con-
> nection between their job performance and the stock's perfor-
> mance, the linkages are all lined up together.
>
> Jack Welch[3]

By focusing on a common set of objectives and measuring performance with data and facts, the barriers between organizations break down. In the old days of
opinions, when it was "their" fault or "if only department
xyz would do their job right," a lot of behavior was driven
by opinions—most of them unfounded. With data-driven
programs, everyone can see their own performance as well

as the performance of others objectively. It is not a matter of doing wrong; rather, it is a matter of recognizing that things are not as good as they should be and taking the challenge to fix it for everyone's success.

The key to a successful Six Sigma program is that it is customer focused. If you think that you know what the customers need, but you haven't verified it with the customers, contact them and make sure that the team is concentrating on the right goals and objectives. Once a team is focused on customer satisfaction, internal conflicts become unnecessary.

Everyone will naturally evolve to doing their jobs differently and better. It becomes a new way of thinking which fuels a rich cultural change. As a culture moves from an atmosphere of employees who come to work encouraged not to think, do what they are told, and leave at the end of the day having performed at the minimal level required to get the job done to an atmosphere where employees are encouraged to use all of their skills, use their mental abilities, constantly think of better ways to do the job, understand the linkage between their performance and the success of the company, and leave at the end of the day knowing that they did their best and that their contribution mattered, the feel of the work environment changes in a very positive way.

I have been involved in several of these transitions, and at some point in the evolution, you walk in one day, and you can feel the energy and camaraderie like static electricity in the air. Those of you who have been similarly involved know that feeling. Those of you who have not yet experienced it are in for a big treat. This metamorphosis affects all employees at all levels.

"I'll believe it when I see it," is wrong. When we understand the impact of our paradigms, we understand that, "I will see it when I believe it."[4]

Work Method Change

The methods and standards for doing work will change. As teams of people become familiar with the power of data, work units will naturally establish charts to monitor their performance. Control charts may be put into place in both manufacturing and administrative operations. Closed-loop feedback systems will be utilized to monitor customer satisfaction levels.

Employees with new knowledge, new skills, and renewed confidence will take both pride and ownership in their performance. These workforces will have some level of empowerment to initiate changes. Empowerment comes with accountability. The teams will understand this and be confident that they can shoulder this new responsibility.

You will find that organizations can be flattened. No one will lose his or her job, but there will be a reassignment of work to get accountability closer to where the work is done. Over time, this reassignment will result in smaller workforces accomplishing more than their predecessors.

Physical Change

As the team studies and analyzes the operation to get to the root cause(s) that is (are) preventing the output to customers from being in line with absolute customer satisfaction, they may discover that the flow of work is problematic. As was illustrated in the flowcharting section in Chapter 6 (Step 3), often the work flow has grown over the years to a point where it no longer makes sense, no one is quite sure why things are being done the way they are other than "we've always done it that way."

Simple physical changes can simplify and streamline an operation. These changes will eliminate unnecessary work and help to mistake-proof the process. Like the example in flowcharting, most administrative processes are rife with unnecessary and redundant operations. Often the required change is to have a department closest to the action perform the task.

Look at your manufacturing flows. Years ago I was involved in the processing of semiconductors. There were eleven steps in the manufacturing flow where product had to go through photo-imaging. Run rates were slow, and mistakes that led to rework were too high. A factory flow study performed on the photo-imaging process revealed that the product queued at several points in the process. It also revealed that on each pass through photo-imaging, the product traveled 2,500 feet. This was within a factory floor space of approximately 50 feet by 75 feet. At almost no cost, one table and one cleaning bench were resituated within the factory. The distance traveled by the product was reduced to 500 feet, and the errors causing rework were reduced from 4 percent to less than 1 percent.

I was also involved with a team that was working on eliminating processing errors within a chemical plant. Partially processed product was getting to the middle of the factory where the errors would be found and the product returned for expensive rework. One of the root problems was that the raw material arrived in the middle of the factory. From there it had to travel east to begin processing. Product in process would then travel west to continue its journey to the end of the line and ultimate delivery to a customer. Of course, as the raw material traveled east and the product in process traveled west, they would bump into each other and some percentage would get mixed. Again, the simple solution was to stage the raw material at the far-east end of the factory so that everything flowed in a continuous journey from east to west.

In a 1960s sit-com titled *The Tycoon,* Walter Brennan played the owner of a manufacturing business, a pragmatic individual who had worked his way to the top with a lot of common sense and a keen understanding of people. In one episode, he could not get the required productivity or quality level out of a line within the factory. He hired four high-powered consulting firms to come up with what was wrong and recommend the required changes. The consulting firm that submitted the winning proposal would get a lucrative contract. All came back with highfalutin ideas that were very expensive, and Walter was not convinced that any of them would work.

Working late one night struggling with how to fix the problem, Walter ran into a young man who was working nights as a janitor while attending college during the day. Walter shared his dilemma with the young man, who agreed to take a look at the problem. The next night he reported that what was needed was a left-handed operator at one of the workstations. Walter implemented the idea, and, as the plot would have it, the problem was solved. That was forty years ago and it was fiction, but the lesson of a little common sense going a long way is timeless.

Required physical changes usually consist of changing the layout of a factory or administrative work flow. Often a simple relocation of one or two workstations is all that is required. Remember all of the Kan-Ban cell manufacturing that was popularized in the 1980s? These were very effective in improving productivity and quality. There are rare occasions when a new piece of equipment may be required.

Procedural Change

Most work flows and operational practices are governed by some form of documented procedure. These have names like standard operating procedure (SOP) or work instructions or processing procedure or department policy. For most companies today, being registered to ISO-9000, or equivalent, is a condition of doing business. These systems all require some form of controlled documentation.

All too often so-called experts write these procedures. These experts come in the form of outside consultants or internal technologists or management representatives. A better way to generate these documents is to have a team comprised of those doing the work and the experts working together to generate the required documents. Thus, a system of continuous improvement teams is the best structure for rooting out less-than-adequate documents and fixing them.

Training

When you are developing your training programs and identifying the required courses, think in terms of what it is that you expect the trainees to do with the new information and skills. An effective training program is well thought out ahead of time, with a clear understanding of how you expect employees to apply the new skills and what improvements in performance you expect to attain.

The best way to train adults is to ask questions instead of giving answers. A group of adult workers has an immense amount of native intelligence that any good trainer taps into and utilizes for the learning of the group. This is all part of instilling the awareness that each of us can contribute more to the success of our operations. When a group of people realize that they are training themselves, they feel a kinship with the new skills. There is no longer a need to ask, "Is this the program of the month?"

The initial training is best done in groups of twenty or less. Some of the subjects, such as the seven tools of problem solving, will take more than one such session. The bulk of the training is what happens after these initial seminars. You must have a cadre of facilitators and coaches ready to lead the transformation process. These people must have the ability to step in and ask the right questions at the right time. They must know how to give feedback working *with* the group rather than talking *to* the group.

Continuous improvement team members require training in problem-solving tools, a logical approach to using the tools, how to work as an effective team member, and how to communicate their activities and achievements. The following chart is one example of a training curriculum for team members.

Required Team Member Training

Subject	Time	Content Overview
Problem-Solving Tools	16 hours	❑ Use a case study. Better yet, use an in-house project. ❑ Present each of the JUSE seven tools of problem solving, and have participants create one example of each.
Six-Step Model	16 hours	❑ Present the model and explain logic of flow. ❑ Stress need to complete each step before proceeding to the next step. ❑ Walk through an example with the participants.
Team Building	16 hours	❑ Discuss different styles. ❑ Provide exercises for conflict resolution. ❑ Present consensus-building techniques. ❑ Practice feedback techniques. ❑ Discuss coaches and champions and how and when to use them. ❑ Present how to manage change. ❑ Provide effective meeting requirements. ❑ Show examples of teamwork and accomplishments. ❑ Demonstrate the importance of listening skills. ❑ Present roles of upper management, middle management, coaches, facilitators, team leaders, and team members.
Effective Presentations	8 hours	❑ Present how to deliver effective presentations. ❑ Discuss how to prepare for different audiences. ❑ Have each participant prepare and present a practice session. ❑ Debrief presentations.

Before you leave Step 5, have you:

❏ Established a method to continue monitoring performance?
❏ Written or amended documents as required?
❏ Completed any required changes to work flow?
❏ Completed all required training?

Notes

1. Kimball Fisher, *Leading Self-Directed Work Teams* (New York: McGraw-Hill, 1993), p. 39.

2. John H. Zenger, Ed Musselwhite, Kathleen Hurson, and Craig Perrin, *Leading Teams* (Burr Ridge, Ill: Irwin, 1994), p. 21.

3. Jean Sherman Chatzky, "GE's Genius Speaks," *USA Weekend*, Sept. 14–16, 2001.

4. Fisher, *Leading Self-Directed Work Teams*, p. 87.

σ

CHAPTER 9

Step 6: Demonstrate Improvement and Celebrate

Back to Focused Metric

The metric that you created in Step 1 is the metric that you have been using throughout the entire root-cause identification and actions to bring performance to an acceptable level. Using this metric, you must demonstrate that you have achieved your goal.

Figure 9-1 illustrates an example of a team that started out with only 10 percent of the documents in their area revised to eliminate the errors causing customer dissatisfaction. They set a goal to have all documents completed within seven months. As their metric shows, they met their goal.

Percent of Documents Revised

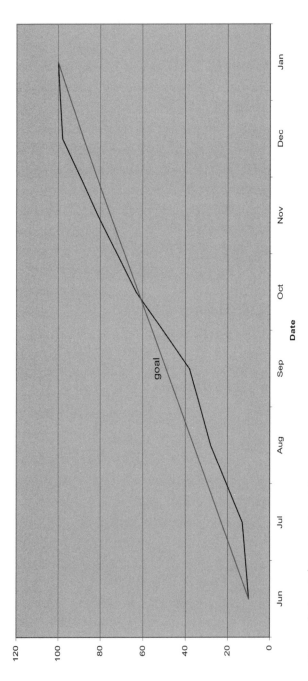

Figure 9-1. Achievement metric.

Success of the Enterprise

The team must demonstrate how their accomplishments contributed to the overall success of the larger enterprise, whether it is a department, a division, a company, or a corporation. Usually, a team must demonstrate how their accomplishments contribute to the success of a company or corporation; however, if a Six Sigma Continuous Improvement program is initiated on a limited basis, such as in one department, then the team's accomplishments can be linked to that department's success. In our example, the team had to explain how revising their documents would contribute to improved customer satisfaction. In this case, the old, out-of-date documents were forcing operators to perform tasks in ways that were not optimal, and they were producing a lot of nonconforming product for their customers. Working in conjunction with other teams within the department that were improving other aspects of the operation, the team was able to show that as they revised the documents, the operators were producing fewer defective parts.

This is why it is important to do the required organizational development work before you initiate a Six Sigma program. The enterprise must have stated and published objectives that guide the activities of the team. Objectives are provided by the senior management of the enterprise. Typical objectives are:

1. Increase market share
2. Reduce manufacturing costs
3. Increase new-product introductions
4. Reduce cycle times for product delivery and service response

5. Zero safety incidents
6. Reduce water and air emissions
7. Improve profit
8. Improve quality in product, service, and administrative functions

Every team must identify at least one such objective that their project is going to positively impact. Tactics are the bottom-up created action plans that are provided by every work unit, division, or department. The teams' operational statement, activities, and action plans become part of the tactics for the enterprise.

In the example of the team that created easy-to-use, correct, and clear documents for the manufacturing of product, their project and actions directly affected several of the typical objectives. When manufacturing is creating defective parts, there is a negative impact on costs, cycle time, and customer-received product. By having a positive impact on the reduction of defective parts, this team is helping to reduce manufacturing costs, reduce cycle times, and improve profits. Thus, at least three of the objectives are germane to the team's efforts.

Reducing the number of defective parts produced will also reduce the number of products that must be reworked. This can have a positive effect on water and ventilation usage; therefore, there could also be a positive effect on the reduction of water and air emissions. Also, when manufacturing is producing defective parts, not all of them are going to be detected internally before they are delivered to the customer; therefore, the team's activities could have a positive impact on improving the quality of the product.

It is extremely important within a Six Sigma program culture that the systems and the people blend together into an integrated unit. Managers must know what employees are doing to contribute to the success of the enterprise, and individual employees must know what they are doing to contribute to the success of the enterprise. This creates a highly effective unit at all levels within an atmosphere of high morale.

Team Recognition

Team recognition is something that must be done throughout the entire course of continuous improvement activities. The most precious thing that you as a senior manager or executive can give is your time. Drop in on a team meeting once in awhile. See what they are working on; give some verbal praise and encouragement. Find out the break schedule for team participants and take a break with them. Ask them what they are working on. Show interest.

One very successful program that I was part of included weekly coaching sessions from the director of operations and the director of quality. We committed from 1 PM until 2 PM every Wednesday afternoon to meet with teams. There was no set agenda. Everyone knew that during that time we would be in a conference room located near the factory floor. Team leaders or entire teams would come in, ask questions, share concerns, and get answers.

Other forms of team recognition include giving each team a bulletin board to display their activities and progress. These bulletin boards should be mounted along a major hallway where most employees pass them at least twice a day. Also, during regularly scheduled monthly communication meetings, schedule five to ten minutes for one or two teams to make a presentation of their project. If you have an internal newsletter, provide a column where team activities and accomplishments can be highlighted.

Team recognition is included here in Step 6 because this is the point where a team has successfully completed a program and achieved the desired results. This is now the point where team members receive formal recognition in front of their peers. The recognition can be scheduled as special stand-alone meetings or as part of regular communication meetings. The important thing is the recognition, not the size or monetary value of the prize; at Motorola we learned that large monetary awards were actually counterproductive.

The best recognition programs consist of small, escalating tokens of appreciation. Programs that I have seen work consist of a series of pins to wear on one's employee badge, such as a yellow ribbon for the first successfully completed program, a red ribbon for the second, and a blue ribbon for the third. Another program that worked was movie tickets for two for each team member every time a Continuous Improvement program was successfully completed.

WARNING: Do not tie the size of the award to the financial impact on the company. This is a recipe for disaster. You may motivate one team, but you are guaranteed to demotivate everyone else. Also, you will discover that every team has at least one budding accountant who wants to question how the financial value was determined.

Besides, this is not what you are striving for. You want everyone engaged in driving improvement throughout the entire enterprise. You do not want to send a message that eliminating typos in work orders is any more or less important than eliminating product defects.

Before you leave Step 6, have you:

- ❏ Received management's approval?
- ❏ Received customer verification that the improvements have taken place?
- ❏ Recognized the team members?
- ❏ Publicized and celebrated the success?
- ❏ Given the team members a token reward?

Getting Started

The considerations for how to initiate the program
required to transition to a Six Sigma culture and how
to effectively manage the change process.

σ

CHAPTER 10

Start Your Journey

Do Something

During the late 1980s there was a meeting within Motorola where a division VP was briefing his staff on the problems that he wanted fixed and projects that he wanted initiated. This was part of the Six Sigma rollout for the division. One of the division staff members said, "Bill, we can't do everything at once." To which Bill replied, "I'm not asking you to do everything at once. (Pause) I am asking you to do something at once."

The staff member's reaction was typical and to be expected. Everyone is busy, and the transition to a Six Sigma system is asking for a lot of change and a lot of new material to learn. How can I be expected to participate in the organizational development, set standards for my department's performance, start tracking defects against those standards, transform defect rate into something called a Sigma value, determine all of the new skills that my people will require, identify the required training, schedule people for training, set aside time each week for people to work on Continuous Improvement programs, share information, change from what I think is a pretty good manager into something they call a leader, and what is a black belt and a green belt anyway? On top of everything else, do I have to start martial arts classes in the evening?

All of the above questions are racing through peoples' heads while they try to absorb all of this new stuff, knowing full well that they will still be expected to keep the product moving, or ship product, or make sales calls or purchase supplies or process accounts receivable, or perform the dozens of other tasks that people do every day to keep the company running.

And, Bill's response was spot-on. The answer is to do something. The point is to start somewhere and to keep building all of the required pieces. Be committed to the fact that this is going to take awhile. There are no magic pills. The adage of eating an elephant one bite at a time applies here. Remember that in order to eat an elephant one bite at a time, you have to start with a first bite.

The Fallacy of Zero Defects

In 1967, I was a crew member aboard the submarine USS *Sam Houston* as she went through the Naval Shipyard in Portsmouth, New Hampshire. The date is significant because it was shortly before this that the USS *Thresher* sank on her shakedown cruise following repair and retrofit in the same shipyard. The *Thresher* went down with all hands. The Navy did scores of what-if tests to try to determine why the *Thresher* sank. I don't know if they ever found an answer that they were 100 percent sure of, but I do know that a lot of our operating systems were improved to encompass a lot of contingencies. The shipyard went on a massive campaign to improve their quality of work.

The first day that we docked in the shipyard, I met a civilian welder who had a huge button about three inches in diameter pinned to the front of his bib overalls. The button was yellow with the letters "ZD" emblazoned on it in bold black type. I asked him what the button was for. He replied, "ZD stands for Zero Defects. I was awarded this button because I didn't make a mistake for a whole year." I was very impressed and congratulated him on his achievement.

I worked with this gentleman for fifteen months. He was a wonder to all of us. He was the most creative person that I have ever experienced. Week after week he could put in forty hours on the job and never do a lick of work. It was amazing to watch him. He would pull his welding cable to some remote corner within the bowels of the ship and sit down with his transistor radio held against the cable, using it as an antenna. For months he did absolutely nothing that could be interpreted as work.

A year passed, and sure enough, he showed up with a huge yellow pin emblazoned with "ZD, 2 years." He had now gone two consecutive years without making a mistake. When you don't do anything, it is easy to not make mistakes or produce faulty product.

Six Sigma is about continually looking for ways to improve your personal performance and your work unit's performance. It has room for making some errors or producing some bad product or performing some service below standard. Precisely, it allows for you to have three defects for every million opportunities that you have to make a mistake. This is a very important tenet of Six Sigma. Besides, unless you produce a gazillion widgets or perform a gazillion tasks every month, three out of a million is virtually zero-defect performance.

When doing the mathematical calculations of dividing

the number of bad products received by customers by the total number of products received by customers, just one defect in the numerator will result in a number much greater than three parts per million. When a similar calculation is done for service or administrative work units, the results will be similar. When dividing the number of unsatisfactory service encounters by the total number of service encounters, one defect in the numerator will result in a number much greater than three parts per million.

So, as you begin your program to transition your operation to one that is governed by Six Sigma, be prepared to make mistakes. If you are like the rest of us, you will make plenty of them. Don't be like our shipyard welder who, in order to make no mistakes, did nothing. Do things, and make your mistakes. When you make a mistake, embrace it. Dissect it and learn what you can from it. They say that mistakes are life's greatest learning opportunities. As enterprises evolve from an okay system to a Six Sigma system, there are many obstacles that need to be overcome. Remember that one of the tenets of Six Sigma is continuous improvement, so don't expect to start off as an expert. As the program grows, lessons will be learned and performance will improve.

The largest challenges are those that each individual must wrestle with in making his or her own personal transition. Everyone will need to learn a new way of looking at how they do their work. Ultimately a successful Six Sigma culture consists of individual employees who apply new thinking and new skills on how to improve their own performance and the performance of the company.

Just as with a program or project, you must set high standards for your personal performance, continually monitor your performance, and take actions to improve your performance. The attainment of Six Sigma is not a destination; the quest for Six Sigma is a never-ending journey.

First Steps

The decision to convert to a Six Sigma culture requires a commitment to do it, and it requires the courage to be prepared to make mistakes. Yes, Six Sigma is a program focused on customer satisfaction that will result in better product and service; however, it is much more than this. It is a cultural change that will affect every employee in the enterprise. People will begin to think differently. They will look at their involvement at work, and at the world in general, with a different perception.

The good news is that form follows function and function follows form. What this means is that you need to provide the rules, models, vision, and structure defining the new form. This newly defined form will enable people to start functioning under the new expectations. Once people begin to function in a new manner and way of thinking, they will then begin to influence the form and evolve it to a higher level. This in turn drives higher levels of functioning, which will then create a higher definition of form. This natural evolution will enable everyone to grow together.

Be prepared for this to take time. Once the leadership of an enterprise has decided that it will convert to a Six Sigma culture, senior management must define when, where, and how it will be done. A vision must be created. Roles and responsibilities must be defined. Accountability methods must be determined. Organizational development work must be completed such that business objects are established and communicated in a manner that will enable the alignment of all subsequent projects to the success of the enterprise. Initial training requirements must be determined. Depending on the size of the enterprise and the scope of deployment, this usually takes from one to three months. Next are the rollout, communication, and training phases. Depending on size, scope of deployment, and resources applied, this usually takes from one to six months. Now the initial projects can be identified and teams established to start the continuous improvement projects.

Typically, it will take individual teams one to two months before achieving any improvement in performance. Teams chartered to improve very complicated or highly technical operations may take longer. Once a team starts to achieve some initial improvement in performance, performance will improve at a high rate. The complexity and scope of most continuous improvement team projects require six months to achieve a Six Sigma level of performance.

Be prepared to stay the course. Programs that are initiated for small enterprises or limited to a small work unit within a large enterprise will begin to see results in three months, and there will be jubilation about outstanding results in about eight months. Programs that are initiated corporatewide at several locations will begin to see results in about a year, and there will be jubilation about outstanding results in about fifteen months (see Figure 10-1).

When creating a Six Sigma culture, it is important to stay focused on the critical components of a Six Sigma

Scope of Six Sigma Program	Time to See Initial Results	Time to See Outstanding Results
Small	3 months	8 months
Large	11 months	15 months

Figure 10-1. Timing for positive return on investment.

1. Customer Satisfaction
2. Decisions Based on Data
3. Continuous Improvement
4. Employee Involvement
5. Financial Improvements
6. Permanence

Figure 10-2. Six foundation stones of Six Sigma.

culture (Figure 10-2). All Six Sigma cultures must start with a focus on customer satisfaction. You must know who your customers are and what it takes to satisfy them. Systems must be established to collect and analyze data. Decisions are made based on data. The program must include team-based continuous improvement projects. Using data analysis techniques, projects will be prioritized and initiated based on customer satisfaction issues and financial considerations. There must be a strong emphasis on employee involvement. Employees from all areas within the enterprise will staff continuous improvement teams. Financial improvements must be realized at all levels. Manufacturing costs should decrease, the time and expense of performing service or administrative functions should improve, profits should improve, and stock prices should improve. Six Sigma must be viewed as a permanent cultural change for the enterprise.

The initial steps required to create a Six Sigma program are:

1. *Decide that you want a Six Sigma culture.* This is not a trivial decision. The decision to create a Six Sigma culture

is going to challenge the way that you have done things in the past. Six Sigma is going to challenge your personal beliefs, and it is going to redefine the rules and expectations for all employees. Some employees will not successfully make the transition; there will be career casualties.

2. *Define and publicize key business objectives.* It is important that you define what your key business objectives are. Once these are established, a system to publicize them must be put in place. Posting them on bulletin boards at key locations throughout the work areas is a good way to do this. Departments or work units must document their objectives in support of the key business objectives. It must be very clear how the activities of each employee group are tied to the success of the enterprise.

3. *Define the new culture.* Depending on the size of the enterprise, the scope of deployment, and the type of business that you are in, successful Six Sigma programs can take different shapes and forms. They all must comply with the six foundation stones of Six Sigma (see Figure 10-2). From this foundation, based on your core values and markets served, create a unique program that best serves your needs. Retail and service companies require a basic set of quality improvement tools focused in logical progression to achieve ever-improving results. In addition to these tools, companies involved in high-tech manufacturing also require advanced techniques for process control, experimental techniques, and data analysis. Other companies serve a customer base, such as the military or automotive manufacturers, with other requirements that must be assimilated into the Six Sigma program. All of this must be considered and articulated into a clear vision of what the new culture will look like.

Some of the old expectations, rules, and standards of acceptable behavior are no longer applicable. These must be expunged from the new culture. New expectations, rules, and standards of acceptable behavior must be determined and incorporated into the new culture description. The description of the new culture provides a 30,000-foot aerial map for everyone to orient against. It must be communicated to all employees. As Yogi Berra said, "If you don't know where you're going, you could wind up someplace else."

4. *Deliver the required training.* Employees within the scope of the Six Sigma culture need to learn new ways of thinking and new skills. As the new culture is defined, you must identify what new behaviors and what new skills are expected of the workforce. Target trainee groups must be identified, and a gap analysis must be completed to identify the required training. A training program must be initiated, a curriculum must be designed, and training must be delivered.

5. *Prioritize key initiatives.* You can't improve everything at once; however, you can begin to improve some things at once. The key is to choose the right things to improve: those things that have the potential for the quickest return on your investments of time, money, and human resources. Measurements of customer satisfaction, internal failures, and financial performance must be determined. If there is no historical data, data must be collected. A Pareto analysis must be completed to identify the major issues. This will determine the charters and make-ups of the initial projects.

6. *Establish macro metrics.* You must determine how you are going to measure the effectiveness of the conversion to Six Sigma. High-level metrics include a way to track the achievement of business objectives. Determine

baseline performance, establish rate-of-improvement goals, and plot your performance to goal. These macro metrics need to be reviewed at least monthly. If you are performing to goal, stay the course. If you are not improving fast enough, rethink and redesign your improvement projects.

7. *Create the initial teams.* Teams must be assigned to all of the prioritized improvement projects. Team leaders, champions, and team members need to be identified. Some projects require work unit teams, and some projects require cross-functional teams. Each team needs to establish a metric for its performance that ties to one of the macro metrics established earlier.

8. *Set up a system to review performance.* Leadership and management people must be held accountable for supporting and deploying the Six Sigma initiatives. Every monthly or quarterly operational review must include a report on how Six Sigma is being utilized. Teams must be held accountable for achieving continuous improvements on measurable results. Management must establish a formal review process that reviews each team's performance on a regular schedule.

9. *Identify coaches and facilitators.* The change required to establish a Six Sigma culture requires people who are spokespersons and role models for the behaviors and skills sets. Coaches are members of senior management that encourage team activities and reinforce positive behaviors. Facilitators are individuals who have an aptitude for Six Sigma, possess excellent interpersonal skills, and are comfortable working in a support role. Facilitators provide guidance for team behaviors and assist teams in the application of quality improvement tools.

10. *Determine how positive team accomplishments will be made visible.* Employees who are participating on teams and achieving positive results in support of the business objectives need to be recognized. A bulletin board where each team can display their project performance should be placed in a central location where all employees are likely to see it. Management must announce the small rewards that are awarded to a team that accomplishes a significant milestone or completes a project. What these rewards are and how they will be publicized need to be included as part of the transition process.

Before and After

It takes a lot of concentrated effort from a lot of people to complete the transition to a Six Sigma culture, and it is worth every step of the way (see Figure 10-3).

Pre-Six Sigma	Post-Six Sigma
Employees perform task by rote	Employees think of better ways to perform tasks
Employees work as individuals	Employees work as team members
Departments work in isolation	Departments work cross-functionally
Focus is internal	Focus is external
Customers' contractual requirements are met	Customers' desires are fulfilled
Customers are satisfied	Customers are thrilled
Quality is inspected in	Quality is built in
Thinking is that things are okay	Thinking is that things need improvement
Many decision are based on opinion	All decisions are based on factual data
Profits are okay	Profits are maximized

Figure 10-3. Pre- and post-Six Sigma.

σ

CHAPTER 11

Managing Change

Overview

The transition from the existing culture within any enterprise to a Six Sigma culture requires three components: leadership, participants, and training. Each of these follows an evolutionary path from initial unfamiliarity with the required knowledge and skills to a mastery of the knowledge and skills. The situation within each enterprise is unique. Some enterprises will already have many of the components required for Six Sigma in place, and some enterprises will be starting from a situation that requires a lot of development. Regardless of the starting point, as the leaders and participants absorb new knowledge, learn new skills, and apply them in a new way of working together, there will be periods of uneasiness.

As it is with the successful implementation of any major initiative, good leadership is crucial. In many existing situations, the leaders and managers must transition from control-centered management to participative leadership. Leaders must be sensitive to the development stages of the employees who are participating in the transition. Knowledge and skills will not be absorbed and effectively utilized instantaneously. As the skill levels of the participants increase, the role of leadership will change.

Coincidental with transitional challenges faced by the leaders, the participants are going through their own transitional challenges. In all cases with which I have been involved, employees were eager to participate in a Six Sigma culture, and they were willing to learn and apply the things necessary to improve their performance. With very few exceptions, people like the idea of working in teams. Having said this, after so many years of working as individuals, the learning process takes time. In the process of evolving from eager anticipation to effective teams, participants go through periods of frustration and adjustment.

The training process from presentation of the new knowledge and skills to the point where the results of the training are realized also is an evolutionary journey. There are too many instances of too many companies spending money on training and never providing an opportunity to use the training, which means that there is no return on the training investment. Training programs must be designed to encompass the transition from being taught skills, to actually learning the skills, to utilizing the skills, to achieving new results by applying the new skills.

Fortunately, each of the three required components— leadership, participants, and training—have existing four-phase models that overlap and intertwine in a complementary manner.

Leadership

The leaders of a Six Sigma transition have two challenges. They have their own personal learning of new skills and new ways of thinking in terms of customer satisfaction and continuous improvement, and they must assist employees in making the same transition. The One-Minute-Manager Situational Leadership II model[1] is an excellent guide for thinking about the development stages of your employees and the changing role of leaders throughout the transition from the existing operating system to a Six Sigma system.

Depending on the development level of individual employees, there are four phases of leadership styles: directing, coaching, supporting, and delegating. The leader's appropriate role changes for each of these phases is illustrated in Figure 11-1.

Participation

The Forming/Storming/Norming/Performing (F/S/N/P) model,[2] shown in Figure 11-2, provides useful insight into what should be anticipated when employees are learning new skills and behaviors within a new culture. The F/S/N/P model provides a roadmap for what to expect in terms of teaming behavior and group effectiveness. Knowing that groups of individuals often start slow and go through a period of misbehaving before they get into an effective work unit will prevent you from becoming discouraged. More importantly, this gives you the opportunity to proactively plan how you will manage through these phases.

Phase	Marked By	Employee Development Level	Marked By	Leader's Role
Directing	-Managers make all decisions -Managers carry all responsibility -Managers hold the information -Workers work by rote -Work is primarily physical, not mental	Low	Enthusiasm	-Provide the training -Develop team expectations -Establish team rules -Model expected behavior -Team is dependent on the leader
Coaching	-Managers solicit suggestions -Responsibility for making goals is shared -Managers share information -Workers provide ideas	Improving	Disillusion	-Facilitate team meetings -Coach individuals -Resolve conflicts -Reinforce positive behaviors -Build trust
Supporting	-Managers collaborate on decisions -Workers make decisions -Workers responsible for results -Workers generate needed information -Workers brief management on progress	Moderate	Reluctance	-Increase challenge -Release some authority -Demonstrate trust -Provide information -Coach the team
Delegating	-Workers are chartered with results -Workers define methods -Workers define work rules -Workers determine roles	High	Competence	-Develop individuals and teams -Publicize successes -Transfer authority to team -Assist with change -Provide recognition

Figure 11-1. Leadership change model.

Phase	Behaviors	Team Performance	Leader's Role
Forming *Testing and Dependence*	-Orientation to the task -Decide on required information -Establishing ground rules -Limits are tested -Hesitant participation -Learning how to learn	-Average Performance -Everyone on Their Best Behavior -Confusion -Wary Acceptance -Rapid Increase in Personal Skills	-Provide the training -Develop team expectations -Establish team rules -Model the behavior -Team is dependent on leader
Storming *Intragroup Conflict*	-Hostility -Expression of individuality -Infighting -React emotionally to the task -Discussion of peripheral issues -Defensiveness -Arguments -Resistance to technique -Polarization -Group unrest	-Declining Performance -Infighting -Interpersonal Conflicts -What's In It For Me? -Resistance to Change	-Facilitate meetings -Coach individuals -Resolve conflicts -Reinforce behaviors -Build trust -Position may be threatened
Norming *Development of Group Cohesion*	-Accept the group -Accept member idiosyncrasies -The group becomes an entity -Strive for harmony -Information is acted on -Common goal identified -Group spirit -Cooperation and mutual support -"We" consciousness	-Performance Hits Bottom & Then Improves -Group Develops Rules of Conduct -Roles are Understood -Conflicts Resolved Quickly -Consensus Building	-Increase challenge -Release some authority -Demonstrate trust -Provide information -Coach the team
Performing *Functional Role-Relatedness*	-Becomes a problem-solving unit -Solutions emerge -The group supports the process -Group freedom -Friendliness -Attainment of the desired goal -Emergence of insight -Collaborative process -Structure is institutionalized -Learn to apply to other situations	-High Levels of Performance -Achievement of Goals -High Morale -Risk Taking -Mutual Trust	-Develop individuals & team -Publicize their successes -Team has authority -Manage change -Reward and recognize

Figure 11-2. Four stages of team development and performance.

Training

People will be expected to think differently, exhibit different behaviors, and apply new skills. To make this transition, they will need training. Kirkpatrick has defined the levels of evaluating the effectiveness of a training program from the training delivery to skills mastery to skills utilization to results from the new skills.[3] These four stages, which are illustrated in Figure 11-3, constitute an evolutionary process that must be incorporated into the design of an effective training program.

A Six Sigma Change Management Model

As we review the phases of the three key components for change—leadership, participation, and training—common themes emerge. From this we can create a comprehensive model for Six Sigma change control management that encompasses all three of these components.

The four phases of the evolution from the initiation of Six Sigma to the successful establishment of Six Sigma as the new culture are:

❑ Phase 1: Definition
❑ Phase 2: Deployment
❑ Phase 3: Growth
❑ Phase 4: Permanence

The required actions and typical behaviors of each phase are listed below:

New Skills Stages	Participant's Need	Activities	Leader's Role
Training in new skills	Must recognize the need to change	- Needs identified - Gap analyses completed - Training program developed - Class curricula created - Training classes held	- Establish method to measure training effectiveness - Publicize training - Communicate expectations - Provide funding
Mastery of new skills	Must know what is expected	- Practice new skills - Deploy skills awareness - Read subject matter books	- Encourage skills usage - Create opportunities for application of skills
Application of new skills	Must be held accountable for application of skills	- Join a team - Seek opportunities	- Establish a formal review system to track usage - Reinforce application of skills
Results from new skills	Must be held accountable for results	- Show positive results - Tie results to business objectives	- Establish a formal system to track results - Provide recognition for effective usage of skills

Figure 11-3. Four stages of effective training program.

Phase 1: Definition

- ❑ Business objectives for the enterprise have been defined.
- ❑ Complete the required organizational development work such that future actions can tie to the business objectives.
- ❑ Define expectations of Six Sigma.
- ❑ Identify the required knowledge and skills.
- ❑ Complete gap analysis between present knowledge and skills and desired knowledge and skills.
- ❑ Determine the required training and initiate the training program.
- ❑ Create the required curricula and begin training.
- ❑ Establish metrics that will measure success of the Six Sigma program.
- ❑ Employees are aware that management is planning a new initiative.
- ❑ At this stage, employee involvement is minimal.
- ❑ Start the training of team leader and facilitator candidates.
- ❑ Employees are both eager and wary of what will be expected of them.
- ❑ Funding is provided for the Six Sigma program.

Phase 2: Deployment

- ❑ The design and expectations of Six Sigma are communicated to all employees.
- ❑ Initial teams are formed and chartered with continuous improvement projects.

❑ Training in teaming skills and improvement tools is provided to all employees.

❑ Leaders begin organizational changes to enable cross-functional and work-unit teams.

❑ Leaders coach individual employees.

❑ Employees are learning new skills and seeking opportunities to apply them.

❑ Facilitators are required for team meetings.

❑ Individual employees realize that it is going to require a lot of personal changes.

Phase 3: Growth

❑ Teams gel as effective continuous improvement units.

❑ Results become rapidly evident as quality improvement tools are applied effectively.

❑ Leaders make more information available to teams.

❑ Leaders are able to transfer responsibility and accountability to the teams.

❑ Formal review processes are in place to monitor the effectiveness of Six Sigma.

❑ As employees not already on teams are making proposals for continuous improvement projects, the number of teams grows.

❑ Facilitators are seldom required at team meetings.

❑ Reflecting a change in the way people view their working relationships and how the work gets done, the everyday language of employees at all levels begins to change.

❑ Morale is improving rapidly.

Phase 4: Permanence

❑ Six Sigma is now the cultural base for the
  enterprise.
❑ Employees think in terms of customer satisfaction.
❑ A mind-set of continuous improvement is
  established at all levels.
❑ Employees at all levels think in terms of collabora-
  tive efforts.
❑ New behaviors and skills have been mastered.
❑ Results continue to soar.
❑ Employees require minimal input from leaders.
❑ Reward and recognition systems are in place to
  reinforce positive results.
❑ Morale is outstanding.
❑ Costs are decreasing and profits are improving.
❑ The enterprise has a positive reputation with
  customers, suppliers, the community, and
  investors.

As a company, division, or work unit transitions along
the journey from the definition phase to the permanence
phase, performance varies (see Figure 11-4). During the
definition phase, before the new skills and behaviors begin
to be rolled out to all employees, the old methods of doing work are still in effect. During this phase, performance
is flat. As the new skills and behaviors are being deployed,
old methods are phased out as employees are struggling
with the application of the new skills. Typically, this can
result in a decrease in performance. Then as everyone
masters the new skills and behaviors, results will soar.

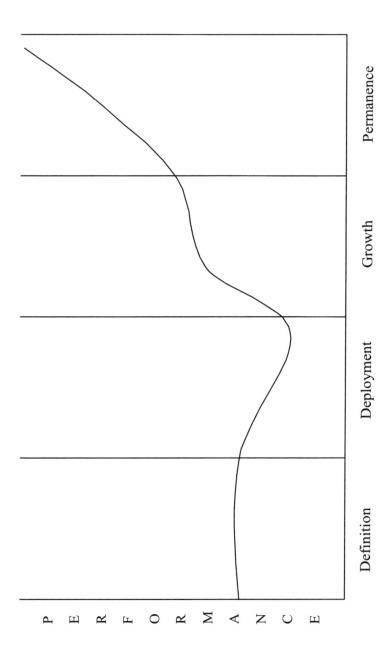

Figure 11-4. Performance levels of Six Sigma transition.

Your Six Sigma Journey

Six Sigma is not a destination; it is a continuous journey. It is a journey that is available to everyone. Whatever your position within the hierarchy of your company, you can participate in the journey. Each journey is unique. I cannot tell you exactly where your journey will take you, but I can tell you that it will be a better place than where you are today.

This book provides the guidelines for how to create a culture where Six Sigma can thrive, how ever-improving results can be achieved by teams that utilize simple tools, and how to work through the changes that will occur along your journey.

Your Six Sigma journey will take you to places where inefficiencies are removed from all operations. Your journey will take you to places where employees of high morale are constantly striving to make things better and are achieving results that were previously unheard of.

Now, please, start your journey.

Notes

1. Kenneth Blanchard, Patricia Zigarmi, and Drea Zigarmi, *Leadership and the One Minute Manager* (New York: William Morrow, 1985).

2. Bruce W. Tuckman, "Developmental Sequence in Small Groups," *Psychological Bulletin* 63, 6 (1965): 384–399.

3. Donald L. Kirkpatrick, *Evaluating Training Programs* (San Francisco: Berrett-Koehler, 1994).

INDEX

accounting, Continuous Improvement programs for, 55

achievement metrics, 150

action, importance of, 159–160

action plans
as components of change management, 31
as living documents, 111
for root cause identification, 108–111

administrative metrics, 55–57

Alice's Adventures in Wonderland, 22–23

"As Is" interdepartmental flowchart, 94, 96–97

"As Is" linear flowchart, 90, 91

"ask why" techniques, 51, 73

attribute data, 60–65
definition of, 60
requirements of, 60
units for measurement of, 61–63

baseline, definition of, 58

baseline performance
as defect rate, 64
metric example of, 65

benchmarking, as quality tool, 22

black belts, 14–15
need for, 33–34

Blanchard Situational Leadership Model, 81

Boyd, L.M., 54

brainstorming
prioritizing of ideas, 105–107
rules of, 99
steps of, 100

Brennan, Walter, 144

business objectives, *see* objectives

champion, role of, 80

change management
components of, 28–31
definition phase, 177
deployment phase, 177–178

change management
  (*continued*)
  growth phase, 178
  permanence phase, 179
  Six Sigma model, 175
charting, *see also* flowcharting
  definition of, 46
  as tool of Continuous
    Improvement, 46
check sheet
  as data collection tool, 112
  definition of, 46
  sample for measurement
    defect, 119–122
  sample for product defect,
    113–116
  sample for product delay,
    116–119
  steps for utilizing, 112–113
closed-ended questions, 35
coaches, *see also* facilitators
  roles of, 168
communication, as Six Sigma
    component, 17, 18
consensus, definition of, 83
continuous data, 58–59
Continuous Improvement
  cycle, 44, 45
  need for, 54–55
  objective of, 50
  teams, *see* teams
  tools
    charting, 88–98
    check sheet, 112–120

fishbone diagram,
    103–105
histogram, 126–130
Pareto diagram, 69–73
scatter diagram, 130–136
stratification, 122–126
Continuous Improvement
    programs
  examples of, 55–57
  initiation of, 68
  institutionalization of,
    138–142
  and physical change,
    142–145
  and procedural change, 145
  and training, 145–147
  and work method change,
    142
Cotter, John, 77
cross-functional mapping, 33
customer data
  collection of, 37
  evaluation of, 34–35
customer nonconformance,
    sample Pareto diagram
    of, 72
customer satisfaction
  as key to Six Sigma pro-
    gram, 141, 165
  survey, 35
  total (TCS), 13, 20
customer service, Continuous
    Improvement programs
    for, 55

data
  analysis tools, *see* histograms; scatter diagrams; stratification
  attribute, 60–65
  collection, 112–113
  tools, *see* check sheet
  continuous, 58–59
  historical, metric example of, 65
  variable, 59
defect rate
  baseline performance as, 64
  calculation of, 61, 62
  metric for, 63
  and Six Sigma calculations, 12
defects, definition of, 57–58
definition, as phase in transition to Six Sigma, 177
Deming, W. Edwards, 19, 23
deployment, as phase in transition to Six Sigma, 177–178
development engineering, Continuous Improvement programs for, 55
DMAIC model, 44
employees
  empowerment of, 22
  pride of ownership of, 15–16

empowerment
  as part of Six Sigma culture, 33
  as quality tool, 22
experimental designs, 59

facilitators
  attributes of, 82
  identification of, 168
  role of, 80–81
  in brainstorming, 99
  as Six Sigma component, 17, 18
Feigenbaum, Armand, 13
financial performance, assessment of, 36
fishbone diagram, 103–105
  and brainstorming, 104
  definition of, 46
  prioritizing of ideas, 105–107
  rules for constructing, 103
  sample, 104
Fisher, Kimball, 139
flowcharting
  interdepartmental, 93–98
  linear, 89–93
  symbols used in, 89
forming/storming/norming/performing model, 172, 174

Galvin, Robert, 7, 9–10
General Electric
    Six Sigma utilization at,
        140
goal, establishment of, 58
green belts, 14–15
    need for, 33–34
growth, as phase in transition
    to Six Sigma, 178

histogram
    creation of, 127–128,
        129–130
    as data analysis tool, 112
    samples, 127–128, 131
    uses for, 126

idea generation, methods of,
    see brainstorming; fish-
    bone diagram
improvement goal
    metric example of, 64, 66
    Six Sigma, 64, 66
improvement metric
    definition of, 57
    elements of, 58
incentive, as component of
    change management,
    29–30
interdepartmental flowchart-
    ing, 88, 93–98
    "As Is," 94, 96–97
    example, 93–98

purpose of, 93
"Should Be," 98, 100–101
inventory control,
    Continuous
    Improvement programs
    for, 56
Ishikawa diagram, see fish-
    bone diagram
Ishikawa, Kauro, 40

Juran, Joseph M., 19

key initiatives, prioritization
    of, 167
Kirkpatrick, Donald L., 175

leadership
    change model, 173
    and Six Sigma transition,
        172
    styles, 172
linear flowcharting
    "As Is," 90, 91
    example, 89–93
    purpose of, 88, 89
    "Should Be," 93, 94
local statistical resources
    (LSRs), 13
macro metrics, 167–168
Malcolm Baldrige National
    Quality Award, com-
    monalities of recipients,
    21

managers
    emergence of new breed
        of, 140
    transition from command-
        and-control orientation,
        139
marketing, Continuous
        Improvement programs
        for, 56
metrics
    administrative, 55–57
    creation of, 63
    definition of, 57
    to illustrate achievement,
        150
    macro, 167–168
    support, 55–57
MIS, Continuous
        Improvement programs
        for, 56
mission statement, definition
        of, 24
Motorola
    benchmarking of Japanese
        operating methods, 8–9
    lessons learned from
        Japanese, 9
    local statistical resources at,
        13
    1980s performance prob-
        lems of, 7–8
    opportunity-for-error
        concept at, 11

Six Sigma launch (1987),
        9
Six Sigma vision statement,
        9, 10
total customer satisfaction
        teams at, 14

negative correlation, as out-
        come of scatter diagram,
        135
Null, Jack, 83

objectives
    definition of, 25
    documentation of, 166
    examples of, 25, 151–152
open-ended questions, 36
operational statement
    criteria for, 50
    definition of, 49
    metric example of, 65
opportunity-for-error
    definition of, 11
    development of concept,
        11
organizational development
    framework for, 24–27
    as key to success of Six
        Sigma, 23–24

Pande, Peter, 12
Pareto diagram

Pareto diagram (*continued*)
    collecting data for, 70–71
    creation of, 71
    definition of, 46, 69
    sub-Paretos, 73
Pareto principle, 69
participation, and transition
    to Six Sigma, 172,
    174
performance
    baseline, *see* baseline per-
        formance
    improving individual,
        162
    measurement of, 58
performance review process,
    establishment of, 168
permanence, as phase in
    transition to Six Sigma,
    179
personnel, Continuous
    Improvement programs
    for, 56
positive correlation, as out-
    come of scatter diagram,
    135
post-Six Sigma culture, 169
pre-Six Sigma culture, 169
prioritizing
    example, 106–107
    techniques for, 105
problem solving, tools of, 45
problem statements, clarity
    of, 50

procedures, Six Sigma effect
    on, 145
process characterization, 59
products, conforming *vs.*
    nonconforming, 60
purchasing, Continuous
    Improvement programs
    for, 56–57

QC Circles, 40
quality assurance,
    Continuous
    Improvement programs
    for, 57
quality control, Continuous
    improvement programs
    for, 57
quality culture
    middle management role
        and, 21
    senior management role
        and, 21
quality programs, evolution
    of, 19, 23

resources, as component of
    change management,
    30–31
reward and recognition
    as quality tool, 22
    as Six Sigma component,
        17, 18
root causes
    definition of, 99

generating lists of, *see*
    brainstorming; fishbone
    diagram
identification of, 108–111
action plans for, 109,
    110
prioritizing of, 105–107

scatter diagrams
    creation of, 131
    as data analysis tool, 112
    definition of, 46, 131
    outcomes of, 135
    samples, 134, 136
scientific approach, used by
    teams, 85
senior executive behavior, as
    Six Sigma component,
    17, 18
service, conforming *vs.* non-
    conforming, 60
"Should Be" interdepart-
    mental flowchart, 98,
    100–101
"Should Be" linear flow-
    chart, 93, 94
Sigma-scale measures, 12
Six Sigma, *see also* Six Sigma
    culture; Six Sigma tran-
    sitioning
    calculations of, 11
    components of, 17, 28
    Continuous Improvement
    program, *see* Con-

tinuous Improvement
    programs
foundation stones of, 165
key to success of, 23
launch of at Motorola, 9
and organizational devel-
    opment, 23–27
rate of improvement goal,
    64
as total quality manage-
    ment system, 20
Six Sigma culture, *see also* Six
    Sigma; Six Sigma transi-
    tioning
articulating a vision of,
    166–167
contents of, 5
creation of, 16–17, 32–34,
    165–169
critical components of, 165
decision to create, 166–167
elements of, 31
evolutionary phases of,
    175, 177–179
ingredients for transforma-
    tion to, 17
success of, 162
Six Sigma program
customer focus of, 141
DMAIC model, 44, 45
increasing participation in,
    43
preliminary steps, 38,
    42–43

Six Sigma transitioning,
    28–31
  definition phase, 177
  deployment phase,
    177–178
  first steps in, 163–169
  growth phase, 178
  performance levels of,
    180
  permanence phase, 179
  pre- *vs.* post-, 169
  training and, 145–147,
    167, 175
skills, as component of
    change management,
    28–29
Smith, Bill
  definition of TQM, 13
  as developer of Six Sigma
    arithmetic, 11, 12
strategies
  definition of, 25–26
  examples of, 26
stratification
  as data analysis tool, 112
  definition of, 46, 122
  examples of, 123–126
sub-Paretos, 73
support metrics, 55–57

tactics, definition of, 26–27,
    152
teaming, *see also* team mem-
    bers; teams

effect of on performance,
    138
  as part of Six Sigma cul-
    ture, 33
  as quality tool, 22
  successful practices of,
    84–85
team leader, role of, 76,
    78–79
team meetings
  reaching consensus in,
    83
  resolving conflicts in,
    83
  rules of conduct for,
    82–84
team members
  defined roles of, 79, 84
  required training for, 146,
    147
  selection of, 73–75
team performance, stages of,
    174
team recognition, 153–155
  importance of, 154
  programs for, 154
team recorder, role of, 79
teams
  balanced participation on,
    85
  Continuous Improvement
    programs for, 55
  creation of, 168
  cross-functional, 37

defined roles on, 79, 84
ground rules for, 85
identification of, 68–73,
    78
improved performance
    due to, 77
membership of, 75–76
    resistance to, 77
motivation of, 74
publicizing accomplish-
    ments of, 169
recognizing knowledge of,
    75
staffing of, 73–77
time commitment of, 76
tooling, Continuous
    Improvement programs
    for, 56–57
total customer satisfaction
    (TCS), 21
    teams, 14
total quality management
    (TQM)
    definitions of, 13
    Six Sigma–based, 20
training
    Continuous Improvement
        programs for, 56–57
    as quality tool, 22
    as Six Sigma component,
        17, 18

and Six Sigma transition,
    145–147, 167, 175
training programs
    design of, 171
    stages of, 176
transitioning, see Six Sigma
    transitioning
Tycoon, The, 144

uniform measurement, as Six
    Sigma component, 17,
    18
USS Sam Houston, 160
USS Thresher, 160

variable data, measurement
    of, 59
vision, as component of
    change management, 28
vision statement, definition
    of, 24

Welch, Jack, 140
work flow, Six Sigma effect
    on, 142–145
work methods, Six Sigma
    effect on, 142
Wycoff, Joyce, 16

zero defects, fallacy of,
    161–162